THE CAMBRIDGE BIBLE COMMENTARY

NEW ENGLISH BIBLE

GENERAL EDITORS

P. R. ACKROYD, A. R. C. LEANEY, J. W. PACKER

JOSHUA

THE BOOK OF
JOSHUA

COMMENTARY BY

J. MAXWELL MILLER

Associate Professor of Old Testament
Candler School of Theology
Emory University

AND

GENE M. TUCKER

Associate Professor of Old Testament
Candler School of Theology
Emory University

CAMBRIDGE UNIVERSITY PRESS

Published by the Syndics of the Cambridge University Press
Bentley House, 200 Euston Road, London NW1 2DB
American Branch: 32 East 57th Street, New York, N.Y. 10022

ISBNS:
0 521 08616 7 hard covers
0 521 09777 0 paperback

First published 1974

Printed in Great Britain
at the University Printing House, Cambridge
(Brooke Crutchley, University Printer)

GENERAL EDITORS' PREFACE

The aim of this series is to provide the text of the New English Bible closely linked to a commentary in which the results of modern scholarship are made available to the general reader. Teachers and young people have been especially kept in mind. The commentators have been asked to assume no specialized theological knowledge, and no knowledge of Greek and Hebrew. Bare references to other literature and multiple references to other parts of the Bible have been avoided. Actual quotations have been given as often as possible.

The completion of the New Testament part of the series in 1967 provides a basis upon which the production of the much larger Old Testament and Apocrypha series can be undertaken. The welcome accorded to the series has been an encouragement to the editors to follow the same general pattern, and an attempt has been made to take account of criticisms which have been offered. One necessary change is the inclusion of the translators' footnotes since in the Old Testament these are more extensive, and essential for the understanding of the text.

Within the severe limits imposed by the size and scope of the series, each commentator will attempt to set out the main findings of recent biblical scholarship and to describe the historical background to the text. The main theological issues will also be critically discussed.

Much attention has been given to the form of the volumes. The aim is to produce books each of which will

be read consecutively from first to last page. The introductory material leads naturally into the text, which
itself leads into the alternating sections of the commentary.

The series is accompanied by three volumes of a more
general character. *Understanding the Old Testament* sets out
to provide the larger historical and archaeological background, to say something about the life and thought of the
people of the Old Testament, and to answer the question
'Why should we study the Old Testament?'. *The
Making of the Old Testament* is concerned with the formation of the books of the Old Testament and Apocrypha
in the context of the ancient near eastern world, and with
the ways in which these books have come down to us in
the life of the Jewish and Christian communities. *Old
Testament Illustrations* contains maps, diagrams and photo-
graphs with an explanatory text. These three volumes are
designed to provide material helpful to the understanding
of the individual books and their commentaries, but they
are also prepared so as to be of use quite independently.

P. R. A.
A. R. C. L.
J. W. P.

CONTENTS

LIST OF MAPS

THE FOOTNOTES TO THE
N.E.B. TEXT

The footnotes to the N.E.B. text are designed to help the reader either to understand particular points of detail – the meaning of a name, the presence of a play upon words – or to give information about the actual text. Where the Hebrew text appears to be erroneous, or there is doubt about its precise meaning, it may be necessary to turn to manuscripts which offer a different wording, or to ancient translations of the text which may suggest a better reading, or to offer a new explanation based upon conjecture. In such cases, the footnotes supply very briefly an indication of the evidence, and whether the solution proposed is one that is regarded as possible or as probable. Various abbreviations are used in the footnotes.

(1) Some abbreviations are simply of terms used in explaining a point: *ch(s).*, chapter(s); *cp.*, compare; *lit.*, literally; *mng.*, meaning; *MS(S).*, manuscript(s), i.e. Hebrew manuscript(s), unless otherwise stated; *om.*, omit(s); *or*, indicating an alternative interpretation; *poss.*, possible; *prob.*, probable; *rdg.*, reading; *Vs(s).*, version(s).

(2) Other abbreviations indicate sources of information from which better interpretations or readings may be obtained.

Aq.   Aquila, a Greek translator of the Old Testament (perhaps about A.D. 130) characterized by great literalness.

Aram.   Aramaic – may refer to the text in this language (used in parts of Ezra and Daniel), or to the meaning of an Aramaic word. Aramaic belongs to the same language family as Hebrew, and is known from about 1000 B.C. over a wide area of the Middle East, including Palestine.

Heb.   Hebrew – may refer to the Hebrew text or may indicate the literal meaning of the Hebrew word.

Josephus   Flavius Josephus (A.D. 37/8–about 100), author of the *Jewish Antiquities*, a survey of the whole history of his people, directed partly at least to a non-Jewish audience, and of various other works, notably one on the *Jewish War* (that of A.D. 66–73) and a defence of Judaism (*Against Apion*).

Luc. Sept.   Lucian's recension of the Septuagint, an important edition made in Antioch in Syria about the end of the third century A.D.

Pesh. Peshitta or Peshitto, the Syriac version of the Old Testament. Syriac is the name given chiefly to a form of Eastern Aramaic used by the Christian community. The translation varies in quality, and is at many points influenced by the Septuagint or the Targums.

Sam. Samaritan Pentateuch – the form of the first five books of the Old Testament as used by the Samaritan community. It is written in Hebrew in a special form of the Old Hebrew script, and preserves an important form of the text, somewhat influenced by Samaritan ideas.

Scroll(s) Scroll(s), commonly called the Dead Sea Scrolls, found at or near Qumran from 1947 onwards. These important manuscripts shed light on the state of the Hebrew text as it was developing in the last centuries B.C. and the first century A.D.

Sept. Septuagint (meaning 'seventy'); often abbreviated as the Roman numeral (LXX), the name given to the main Greek version of the Old Testament. According to tradition, the Pentateuch was translated in Egypt in the third century B.C. by 70 (or 72) translators, six from each tribe, but the precise nature of its origin and development is not fully known. It was intended to provide Greek-speaking Jews with a convenient translation. Subsequently it came to be much revered by the Christian community.

Symm. Symmachus, another Greek translator of the Old Testament (beginning of the third century A.D.), who tried to combine literalness with good style. Both Lucian and Jerome viewed his version with favour.

Targ. Targum, a name given to various Aramaic versions of the Old Testament, produced over a long period and eventually standardized, for the use of Aramaic-speaking Jews.

Theod. Theodotion, the author of a revision of the Septuagint (probably second century A.D.), very dependent on the Hebrew text.

Vulg. Vulgate, the most important Latin version of the Old Testament, produced by Jerome about A.D. 400, and the text most used throughout the Middle Ages in western Christianity.

[. . .] In the text itself square brackets are used to indicate probably late additions to the Hebrew text.

(Fuller discussion of a number of these points may be found in *The Making of the Old Testament* in this series.)

THE BOOK OF
JOSHUA

✳   ✳   ✳   ✳   ✳   ✳   ✳   ✳   ✳   ✳   ✳   ✳   ✳

THE BOOK AS LITERATURE, HISTORY AND THEOLOGY

The central theme of the book of Joshua is the acquisition of
the land of Canaan by the people of Israel under the leadership
of Joshua, the successor of Moses. That acquisition includes the
conquest of the land west of the river Jordan and the division
of the territory among the individual tribes. But the book of
Joshua is a complex and often puzzling one. Its meaning cannot
be captured by describing its major theme. That theme itself
has numerous motifs; some parts seem to contradict others,
and the passage of time has obscured the meaning of many
words and sentences and paragraphs, leaving the contem-
porary reader with numerous questions.

Certain of these are preliminary questions which we must
raise concerning any book from antiquity, and especially one
so ancient and complicated as the book of Joshua. For the sake
of clarity they may be raised under three headings: literary,
historical, and theological questions. These headings are,
admittedly, somewhat arbitrary since all the questions touch
one another and at many points they overlap. We cannot, for
example, determine the historical accuracy of the story without first understanding the book as literature, nor can we fully
grasp the book's religious ideas without understanding how it
was composed from different literary documents and oral
traditions. On the other hand, historical and theological in-
sight is required in order to answer the literary questions
themselves.

The literary questions include inquiries concerning authorship, date, outline and contents, genres (or types) of literature,

and – in this case as in many others in the Old Testament – the investigation of the oral traditions which preceded and to some extent paralleled the writing of the book. In other words, what are the literary characteristics of the book, and what was its literary – and pre-literary – history? In raising the historical questions we shall want to learn what we can concerning the events which this book sets out to describe, namely, the Israelite conquest of Palestine. To what extent is this book a reliable source for that history? By raising theological issues we acknowledge that this book, after all, not only comes to us as a document of more than one religious faith, but that it also *arose* as an expression of faith. What, then, is the theological and religious significance not only of the major theme of the book, but also of the subordinate motifs?

So it is necessary to raise many questions, to look at the material in the book of Joshua from different perspectives, and to characterize it in various ways. But the purpose of all such inquiries and descriptions is to lead directly back to the text itself, for that is the real focus of our interest.

LITERARY PROBLEMS

The literary context of the book and the question of authorship

The Old Testament itself preserves no tradition concerning the authorship of the book of Joshua. It is an anonymous work, as are all the other narrative books of the Old Testament. 'Joshua' is the title of the book, not the name of its writer. The title is derived from the main character in the story, who emerges at the beginning as the successor to Moses, having been designated earlier, and at the end, having said his farewells, dies and is buried. The principle which was followed in establishing the title, then, is the same that was followed with regard to the books of Judges, Samuel, and Kings.

The anonymous character of the book reflects a significant fact which is confirmed by critical scholarship: the book is *not* the work of a single author. Rather, it is a composite work which is the result of a long history of composition. The variety of literary styles and genres, the presence of contradictions and duplicates and some variations in historical and theological perspective suggest that the contributions to this book were many. Some of these originated as written documents, but others arose as oral traditions, circulating perhaps for centuries before they were written down. The question of 'authorship' must thus be replaced by the much more complicated question of the history of the growth and composition of this book, from the earliest discernible stages to its final form.

First we must examine the literary and traditional context to which the book belongs. At least in terms of its content and themes, the book of Joshua is properly the link between the Pentateuch (Genesis to Deuteronomy inclusive) and the historical books which begin with Joshua and continue to the end of 2 Kings. (In the Hebrew Bible the book of Ruth is not placed after the book of Judges.) This fact lies at the root of many of the problems of authorship and literary history: is it to be understood as the final chapter of the story begun in Genesis, and its literary problems resolved by methods which have been found useful for the Pentateuch, or is it to be regarded as a part of the 'historical books', and its literary history interpreted in that context?

On the one hand the book of Joshua reports the completion of the theme which is initiated as early as Gen. 12: 1–3, the promise of land to the descendants of the patriarchs. But on the other hand it is the beginning of the account of Israel's history in the land of Canaan. In the Hebrew canon the book definitely was associated more directly with the historical books than with the Pentateuch. It belongs to the second division of the canon, the Prophets, as the first of the 'Former Prophets'. The divisions made by the canon are, however, quite late and in some cases artificial. The first five books were the first to be recognized as holy scripture, primarily because special significance was attached to the giving of the law by

Moses. Hence as a collection they are called 'the Torah' (the Law), and individually identified as 'books of Moses', that is, *concerning* Moses.

When critical scholarship in the last part of the nineteenth century described the making of the Pentateuch in terms of a series of literary documents it also recognized the continuation of the Pentateuchal themes into the book of Joshua and thus analysed the latter by the same principles. The 'Documentary Hypothesis', which saw the Pentateuch as composed of four main sources, J, E, D, and P (the Yahwist, the Elohist, Deuteronomy, and the Priestly document; see *The Making of the Old Testament* in this series, pp. 6off.), was extended to Joshua, and usually also to Judg. 1: 1 – 2: 5. Until recently this represented the dominant critical view concerning the book of Joshua, and some scholars still argue strongly that a modified version of that hypothesis should be applied to this book.

However, more recent studies have forced a reassessment of that analysis and resulted in what appears to be a more reasonable understanding of the literary history of the book. In the first place, the specific literary and linguistic similarities between the material in Joshua and that in the narrative sources of the Pentateuch cannot be demonstrated convincingly. And such literary affinities were, after all, the primary basis on which the narrative sources were distinguished from one another. At the very most there are remnants or traces of such sources in the book of Joshua, but even that appears doubtful. Certainly no continuous narrative strands which would represent the concluding chapters of J, E, or P can be recovered.

Second, while the presence of the narrative sources of the Pentateuch cannot be demonstrated conclusively, it is agreed almost unanimously by scholars that a great deal of the material in the book of Joshua parallels the style and the point of view of *one* of the Pentateuchal sources: Deuteronomy. Very close literary and theological affinities with Deuteronomy (i.e.

words, phrases and ideas) can be recognized in whole chapters (e.g. Josh. 1 and 23) as well as in scattered paragraphs and verses.

The fact that similar materials are found throughout the Former Prophets has led to the conclusion that the books of Deuteronomy, Joshua, Judges, 1 and 2 Samuel, and 1 and 2 Kings comprise a single history written in the style and from the theological perspective of Deuteronomy. Though it is based upon and incorporates diverse traditions from various periods, it now stands as a single work, the history of Israel from the time of Moses to the Babylonian captivity.

Many questions concerning this Deuteronomistic history have not been resolved. Is it the work of a single writer, or the work of a school? Similarly, was there only a single edition of the work, or a series of editions? (It now seems most likely that there were at least two editions of the work.) There are disagreements concerning the purpose of the history, turning in part upon the answers to the above questions. However, the date of its final writing, the basic principles of its composition, and the place of the book of Joshua in the whole work are relatively clear.

The history certainly was written after – but not long after – the last event it reports, the release of Jehoiachin, the last Judaean king, from prison during the Babylonian exile. It thus should be dated about 550 B.C. The Deuteronomistic historian (or historians) was a 'redactor' in the proper sense of the term; that is, he did not invent this story but assembled old written and oral traditions into a coherent – if not always consistent – unity. He provided an interpretative framework which not only linked the older materials together but also presented his judgements concerning the events reported. He revised some of the materials at hand, and also supplied some speeches and narratives which he himself composed. Among the materials at his disposal were the books which he refers to by title (e.g. 'the Book of Jashar', Josh. 10: 13, 2 Sam. 1: 18; 'the annals of the kings of Israel', 2 Kings 15: 21) and

numerous other unidentified works. These sources included
such diverse materials as annals, records, king lists, and stories
of various kinds. Some of the materials doubtless had already
reached the form of collections or compositions, for example,
the story of the later life of David (2 Sam. 9–20, 1 Kings 1–2)
and the stories about Elijah and Elisha. The historian also
incorporated an earlier version of the book of Deuteronomy,
which he supplied with a new introduction and conclusion.
The book of Joshua is the second chapter in the Deuteronomistic history.

Outline of the contents

The literary characteristics of the book of Joshua and its
structure have been determined by this last fact. But, as we
have seen, the Deuteronomistic historian did not invent his
story, but rather composed it from older written and oral
traditions which also influenced his work. Before examining
the traditions which the historian used in this particular book
we should analyse its contents and structure. Though the book
contains speeches and lists and descriptions of the territory of
Israel, its structure from beginning to end is that of a narrative;
that is, it reports events from the perspective of a third person,
it characterizes the main actors in the drama, and it follows a
plot which develops to a climax.

The contents may be outlined as follows:

1. *Israel's entry into the promised land* (1–12)
    A. Introduction (1)
    B. The spies sent to Jericho (2)
    C. The crossing of the Jordan and the events at Gilgal (3–5)
    D. The conquest of Jericho (6)
    E. The Achan story and the conquest of Ai (7 – 8: 29)
    F. A ceremony on Mount Ebal (8: 30–5)
    G. The treaty with the Gibeonites (9)
    H. The battle with the five Amorite kings and the southern
       campaign (10)
    I. The northern campaign (11: 1–15)

J. General summary, including a list of conquered kings
    (11: 16 – 12: 24)

2. *The division of the land among the tribes* (13–22)
    A. Introduction: The description of the unconquered lands
        and the territory of the tribes beyond the Jordan (13)
    B. The portions of three tribes (14–17)
    C. The portions of the seven other tribes (18–19)
    D. Special cities: The cities of refuge and the Levitical
        cities (20–1)
    E. The return of the trans-Jordanian tribes and the question
        of their altar (22)

3. *Joshua's farewell and death* (23–4)
    A. The last words of Joshua (23)
    B. The assembly at Shechem (24: 1–28)
    C. The graves of Joshua, Joseph, and Eleazar (24: 29–33)

The Deuteronomistic historian and the older traditions

The outline of the contents itself suggests two factors of significance for the history of the book: on the one hand, it
includes a great many diverse traditions, but on the other hand
these traditions are ordered into a more or less systematic
unity. Our task at this point is to distinguish between the
contributions of the editor and those pre-Deuteronomistic
traditions. It is hardly possible to reconstruct all the stages in
the development of the book, but some of the main blocks
used in composing the work can be recognized.

Several large units are to be attributed in their entirety to
the Deuteronomistic redactor. They are: 1; 12; 21: 43 – 22: 6;
and 23. In each of these units the parallels to the style, language,
and theology of the book of Deuteronomy are numerous and
clear. (See the commentary for details.) This material consists
in great measure of speeches (1; 22: 1–5, 8; 23) and summaries
which either introduce (1) or conclude (12; 21: 43–5; 23)
stages in the account. There are numerous other smaller con-

tributions by the Deuteronomistic historian, many of which also provide the connecting links between the parts of the story.

Ch. 24 presents special problems. It seems to consist of old traditions which have been thoroughly reworked by the redactor. In one sense it parallels ch. 23 – both purport to give the last speech of Joshua – and in another sense it parallels 8: 30–5 – both report a covenant ceremony at Shechem. These parallels have led some scholars to suggest that there were two distinct Deuteronomistic editions of the book. That is quite possible, but it is very difficult to distinguish between different stages of Deuteronomistic style.

At first glance the summaries might lead one to believe that the first part of the book (1–12) reports the conquest of the entire land of Canaan west of the Jordan. But closer reading of the individual stories presents a different picture. Those stories do not deal with the conquest of the entire land at all; the events they report are concentrated in the territory of one tribe and revolve around one place. The place is the old sanctuary at Gilgal and the tribe is Benjamin. The crossing of the Jordan (3–4) is near Gilgal, where the people established their first camp (4: 19–24). Gilgal was the site of the first celebration in the promised land (5), and Jericho apparently was in the immediate vicinity (2; 6). When the tribes first moved out of the Jordan valley they took the cities in the central hill country in the territory traditionally assigned to the tribe of Benjamin (7; 8; 10: 1–27). So the main body of tradition in the first part of the book concerns the tribe of Benjamin, and probably was once handed down – and preserved at the sanctuary at Gilgal – as the report of the way that particular tribe acquired its land. The other main stories in the first part of the book report the southern expedition (10: 28–43) and the conquest of the north (11: 1–23). However, even these traditions about the non-Benjamite territory have been related to the stories concerning Gilgal and Benjamin.

In terms of their literary type or genre a great many of the individual stories in this first part of the book are aetiological stories; that is, they explain the existence of a present phenomenon by reference to an event in the past. Thus the name 'Gilgal' is explained in terms of the first circumcision in Palestine (5: 2–9), the story of the spies sent to Jericho explains the preservation of the family of Rahab the prostitute (2; 6: 22–5), and the 'Vale of Achor', or 'valley of Trouble', was so named because it was there that Achan brought trouble on Israel (7: 24–6). Some scholars have argued that questions about origins (aetiological questions such as, 'when your children ask you what these stones mean', 4: 6) in most cases created such stories, that is, that the stories were created as answers to the questions. Certainly many of the stories in this book have aetiological conclusions (e.g. 'Therefore the place is called Gilgal to this very day', 5: 9), but it is difficult to determine whether the question about the origin of a name or the like created the story or the account depends upon an accurate historical memory. Some have argued that in most cases the aetiological conclusion was a secondary development in the tradition, but the literary character and the historical reliability of each story must be examined individually.

The main traditions which underlie the second part of the book (13–22) are lists of various kinds. Until relatively recently most scholars regarded these lists as very late exilic or post-exilic idealizations of the land of Israel. But now it seems much more probable that some of these lists do in fact relate to actual stages in the geographical organization of Israel. There are two main kinds of lists here: town lists and boundary lists. The town lists (see Map 3) simply enumerate the cities belonging to various tribes. Twelve groups of towns are given, but though there were twelve tribes the town groups do not always correspond to the tribal holdings. Only the cities in the southern part of Palestine are given. The town lists apparently gave administrative districts as they were organized during the Israelite monarchy, probably in the time of Josiah (640–609 B.C.). Some, however, have dated the lists in the time of earlier kings.

The boundary lists on the other hand (see Maps 4 and 5) describe a line, the border between the individual tribes. The line is traced on a map: 'It started from the Edomite frontier at the wilderness of Zin and ran as far as the Negeb at its southern end, and it had a common border with the Negeb at the end of the Dead Sea, where an inlet of water bends towards the Negeb. It continued from the south...' (15: 1ff.). Most scholars now are agreed that the boundary lists give an ancient map of Israel from the time of the judges, not long after the conquest. While this map may not have described the actual tribal holdings, it at least stated the claims of the individual tribes, and thus served as the basis for arbitration of conflicts among them. But we must bear in mind that even if these lists are old, we must still carefully consider the reason why they have been preserved and how they have been used in the work as a whole.

The major old tradition in the third part of the book is the pre-Deuteronomistic material in ch. 24, the report of the renewal of the covenant at Shechem. There is abundant evidence that this account reflects an institution of great importance and great antiquity in Israel.

HISTORICAL PROBLEMS

Why cannot we simply recite the story as it is told in the book of Joshua as the history of the conquest? There are many reasons. First, there are inconsistencies and contradictions within that story itself. Some of these appear to be minor points, but even they begin to show the difficulties. For example, after the crossing of the Jordan, was the monument set up 'in the middle of the Jordan at the place where the priests stood' (4: 9), or near the river 'in the camp where you spend the night' (4: 3)? And how many men did Joshua send to wait in ambush before the second attack on Ai, thirty thousand (8: 3), or five thousand (8: 12)? More serious are the conflicts between chs. 1–12 and Judg. 1: 1 – 2: 5. The former seem to talk about violent warfare by all Israel while the latter picture the individual tribes or clans taking their own territory and settling alongside Canaanites. In addition to the difference of perspective in these two units, some of the conquests in Judg. 1 had already been reported in Josh. 1–12.

Second, there are problems created by the character and date of the narrative itself. The book in its final form stems from the Babylonian exile, more than 500 years after the events which it reports. Significant portions of the book actually were written by the Deuteronomistic historian at that time. His writing is deeply influenced by his own particular theological outlook and interpretation. Furthermore, while he may have employed some materials which reliably record the events, he also incorporated legends as well as administrative documents from the time of the Israelite monarchy.

Third, one cannot simply recite the account in the book of Joshua as the history of the conquest because there are additional data to be considered. This includes other material within the Old Testament. Especially important are the contributions from the book of Judges. The account in Judg. 1: 1 – 2: 5, which apparently is very old, has been mentioned already. Among the other relevant materials is Gen. 34, the story of the rape of Dinah, the alliance with the citizens of Shechem, and the attack on the city by Simeon and Levi. This account perhaps reflects the first attempt by those two tribes to settle in the region of Shechem. Still other evidence comes from the archaeological exploration of the ancient Near East. This includes relatively few written documents or inscriptions, but a great wealth of material remains from sites in Palestine.

Thus we must critically evaluate all the evidence at our disposal before suggesting a reconstruction of the conquest. Certain principles will guide the analysis of the evidence and the writing of a history. It is a sound principle of historical

reconstruction that – all other things being equal – the older
the document, or the nearer it is to the events under consideration, the more reliable it is. Unfortunately, however,
'all other things' seldom are equal. While the ideal source is
one which comes from the time of the events, other factors
must be taken into consideration. Among these is the question
of the literary type of the documentary evidence: annals,
lists, and other official documents tend to preserve data more
accurately than do legends or popular tales. Moreover, the
perspective or bias and purpose of each source must be
evaluated. Even sources close to the events will select and
order what they report.

By these principles the book of Joshua has severe limitations
as evidence upon which to base historical reconstruction.
Much of the material is too late to be very reliable: the
Deuteronomistic framework tells us more about the ideas of
the late monarchy and the exile than it does about the events of
the conquest. The older traditions doubtless preserved many
accurate memories, but it is always difficult and often impos-
sible to distinguish the reliable from the unreliable. Certainly
the most useful historical tradition is the list of tribal boundaries in the second part of the book. But even that list reflects
the situation after the conquest, when all the tribes were
settled in the land of Palestine. In order to venture any historical judgements at all we must look at each of the traditions
in the light of all the evidence at our disposal.

The biblical tradition must be examined in the light of the
archaeological evidence. Excavations in recent decades have
established beyond a reasonable doubt that many Palestinian
cities were destroyed in the second half of the thirteenth
century B.C. These include some of the cities reportedly
defeated by Joshua. The evidence seems quite conclusive with
regard to Hazor (11: 11, 13), Bethel (12: 16) and Lachish
(10: 32). There is, of course, no archaeological proof that
invading Israelites were responsible for these destructions,
but they do coincide with the most probable date for the

conquest. Furthermore, at a number of sites – including some in the Jordan valley and Hazor – there is evidence of cultural change immediately following the period of the destruction. Many archaeologists have seen in the successive layers of debris evidence of Canaanite occupation followed by massive destruction. They interpret the very poor occupation levels after the destruction as Israelite settlement which dates before the time of the Philistines. However, the pattern of cultural change is far from certain – it was a time of considerable unsettlement generally. More important, we must recognize that to identify the various stages with one group or another requires our interpretation of the evidence.

Furthermore, while some evidence seems to coincide with accounts in the book of Joshua, other excavations have produced results which are at variance with the biblical tradition. This includes, for example, Megiddo which seems to have been destroyed in the last part of the thirteenth century. The king of Megiddo is listed as one of those conquered by Joshua (12: 21), but elsewhere (Judg. 1: 27) it is explicitly stated that the city was not captured: the Canaanites held their ground in that region. Even more dramatic are the results of the excavations at Jericho and Ai. The book of Joshua contains extensive stories concerning the destruction of these two cities. But at Jericho there is no evidence for occupation after the fourteenth century B.C., and Ai had been a ruin for more than 1000 years before the Israelites arrived in Canaan. Thus while archaeology has made significant contributions to the understanding of the period of the Israelites' entry into Palestine, it cannot be stated uncritically that the excavation of Palestinian cities supports the historical reliability of the Old Testament narratives.

What, then, can the historian say concerning the events reported in the book of Joshua? At the outset it must be acknowledged that the present account is a schematic, simplified, and incomplete report of Israel's occupation of her homeland. The story has been influenced significantly by the theological views of those who handed it down. For instance, it was generally assumed that all Israel was directly involved in all these significant events, but evidence tends to suggest that in fact 'all Israel' did not exist until after the individual tribes had settled in Palestine. It is thus no longer possible to reconstruct in detail either the sequence of events or the specific groups or individuals involved at each particular stage. However, some generalizations are justified. The account in Judg. 1, the tribal character of most of the individual stories in Josh. 2–10, and the old map of tribal claims all suggest that the individual actions – migrations and wars – of the individual tribes, at times acting in concert with other tribes, were basic. The Israelite settlement in Palestine probably was a long process of occupation (13: 1–7; 23: 6–13). The evidence for the destruction of Palestinian cities in the second half of the thirteenth century B.C. suggests that there were violent phases to this occupation. However, one cannot attribute every destruction in this period to the Israelites, since other groups also were involved in Palestinian campaigns at approximately the same time, including Egyptian pharaohs and the Sea Peoples, among whom were the Philistines.

THEOLOGICAL ISSUES

A book which is the result of a long history of growth and composition should also reflect a long history of theological reflection. This is true only to a limited extent with regard to the book of Joshua. The voice of the Deuteronomistic historian is so strong here that in most instances all that remains of older ideas are echoes. Certainly there are traces of old religious institutions and ideas, but most of the self-conscious theological reflection is the work of the final redactor. In summarizing the main themes of the book, we shall recognize that most of them are consistent with the outlook of Deuteronomy, but we shall also attempt to recognize the older roots of those themes and ideas.

The central theological statement is that the LORD has fulfilled his promises to the forefathers of Israel by granting a land
to their descendants. We should consider first the relationship
of this theme to the message of the Deuteronomistic history
as a whole and then examine some of its ramifications.

The basic purpose of the Deuteronomistic history as a whole
was to interpret the disaster of the Babylonian exile in terms
of the past. The writer justified God's judgement by pointing
to what he understood as a history of sin. He measured
Israel's behaviour – and in particular that of the kings of
Israel and Judah – by the understanding of the law presented
in the book of Deuteronomy, and found it wanting. The
theme of disobedience and rebellion actually begins in Judg. 2.
The first two 'chapters' of the story (Deuteronomy and
Joshua) laid the foundation. They report the giving of the
law, the establishment of the covenant and the LORD's fulfilment of his promise. The era under Joshua's leadership is
presented somewhat nostalgically as a time of faithfulness and
obedience. This period could be interpreted so positively in
part because God was directly at work performing an act of
grace on behalf of his people, but also because Joshua – unlike
most of the kings who were to follow – was the proper leader,
the legitimate successor to Moses.

There are other themes in the Deuteronomistic history. In
one sense it might appropriately be termed the history of the
word of the LORD. Just as the book of Joshua reports the
fulfilment of an old promise, so many of the disasters in
Israel's history are interpreted as fulfilments of previous
announcements. There are correlations between prophetic
announcements of judgement and their fulfilments. Thus the
title 'Former Prophets' given to these books in the Hebrew
Bible is not inappropriate. There is also a note of hope throughout this work. This is implied in the numerous exhortations
to faithfulness, in the promise of an everlasting dynasty to
David (2 Sam. 7), and in the work's final paragraphs, which
report the release from prison of the last Judaean king. Perhaps

one function of the book of Joshua in this context is to remind
the exiles that the land which they have lost is theirs by the
promise, and they may regain it. That point, however, is
never made explicit.

Only in a limited sense is the story of the acquisition of the
land an account of human activity. The people of Israel moved
from conquest to conquest over the native population and
then the land was parcelled out among the tribes. At the end
of the story the LORD reminds Israel: 'I brought you into the
land of the Amorites...I destroyed them for your sake'
(24: 8). Throughout the book the battles are understood as
'holy war', in which rigid adherence to the cultic regulations –
that is, performance of the proper rituals – was more important than tactics and force of arms. Walls crumbled at the
sound of a trumpet and a shout, and when additional daylight
was needed the sun stood still. In short, as the LORD reminds
the people: 'I spread panic before you, and it was this, not
your sword or your bow, that drove out the two kings of the
Amorites. I gave you land on which you had not laboured,
cities which you had never built; you have lived in those
cities and you eat the produce of vineyards and olive-groves
which you did not plant' (24: 12–13). That this view of the
conquest is not limited to the book of Joshua is seen by references in Israel's songs of worship:

> O God, we have heard for ourselves,
>   our fathers have told us
> all the deeds which thou didst in their days,
> all the work of thy hand in days of old.
> Thou didst plant them in the land and drive the nations out,
> thou didst make them strike root, breaking up the peoples;
> it was not our fathers' swords won them the land,
> nor their arm that gave them victory,
>   but thy right hand and thy arm
>   and the light of thy presence; such was thy favour to
>   them. (Ps. 44: 1–3)

It may seem rather strange to make theological statements, that is, statements about God and his nature and purpose, by recording and reading lists of cities and boundaries. Nevertheless, we must appreciate the theological significance of such materials in this book. Tribal boundaries and administrative organizations doubtless served a real political and social need. But at the same time they are seen here as effecting what was considered a divinely ordained structure of life for Israel, established by God's acts of salvation. Salvation here means not primarily some personal spiritual experience, but refers to historical, political and even geographic realities. So the LORD not only gave Israel a land, but also organized the lives of the tribes in it.

The book's final chapter also relates to the ordering of Israel's life. In the covenant renewal ceremony, which is centuries older than the Deuteronomistic historian, the tribes pledge their loyalty to one another and to their God. The meaning, and even the continuation, of Israel's life will turn on her faithfulness to those promises.

A NOTE ON GEOGRAPHY

The book of Joshua contains a very large number of place-names. Some of these are well known from other parts of the Old Testament and from their subsequent existence; but there are many which appear only here or which even if mentioned elsewhere are difficult to identify with any certainty. Much of the more detailed discussion, particularly of chs. 13–21, depends on geographical factors and the identification of places. The commentary contains some discussion of the many complex issues. To assist the reader further a Gazetteer has been added (pp. 189–200); this, together with the maps, provides much further information both about the problems of identification and about the degree of certainty which appears to be available. There is also on pp. 186–8 a short list of the main geographical terms used in the book of Joshua.

✳   ✳   ✳   ✳   ✳   ✳   ✳   ✳   ✳   ✳   ✳   ✳   ✳

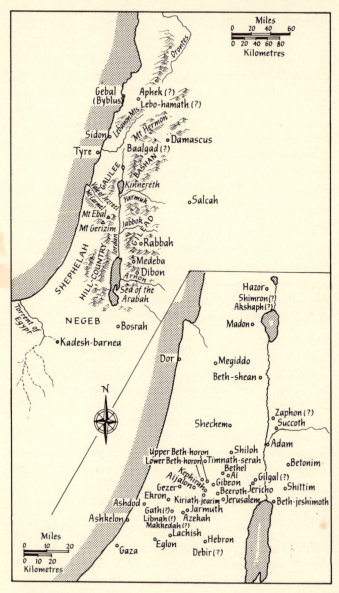

1. Topography of Syria–Palestine and sites mentioned in chs. 1–11. See Gazetteer.

18

Israel's entry into the promised land

THE PREPARATIONS

AFTER THE DEATH of Moses the servant of the LORD, **1**
the LORD said to Joshua son of Nun, his assistant, 'My **2**
servant Moses is dead; now it is for you to cross the
Jordan, you and this whole people of Israel, to the land
which I am giving them. Every place where you set foot **3**
is yours: I have given it to you, as I promised Moses.
From the desert and the Lebanon to the great river, the **4**
river Euphrates, and across all the Hittite country westwards to the Great Sea,*ᵃ* all this shall be your land. No **5**
one will ever be able to stand against you: as I was with
Moses, so will I be with you; I will not fail you or forsake
you. Be strong, be resolute; it is you who are to put this **6**
people in possession of the land which I swore to give to
their fathers. Only be strong and resolute; observe dili- **7**
gently all the law which my servant Moses has given you.
You must not turn from it to right or left, if you would
prosper wherever you go. This book of the law must ever **8**
be on your lips; you must keep it in mind day and night
so that you may diligently observe all that is written in it.
Then you will prosper and be successful in all that you
do. This is my command: be strong, be resolute; do not **9**
be fearful or dismayed, for the LORD your God is with
you wherever you go.' Then Joshua told the officers to **10,11**
pass through the camp and give this order to the people:
'Get food ready to take with you, for within three days

[a] *Or* the Mediterranean Sea.

you will be crossing the Jordan to occupy the country
12 which the LORD your God is giving you to possess.' To
the Reubenites, the Gadites, and the half tribe of Manasseh,
13 Joshua said, 'Remember the command which Moses the
servant of the LORD gave you when he said, "The LORD
your God will grant you security here and will give you
14 this territory." Your wives and dependants and your
herds may stay east of the Jordan in the territory which
Moses has given you, but for yourselves, all the warriors
among you must cross over as a fighting force at the head
15 of your kinsmen. You must help them, until the LORD
grants them security like you and they too take possession
of the land which the LORD your God is giving them.
You may then return to the land which is your own
possession,*a* the territory which Moses the servant of the
16 LORD has given you east of the Jordan.' They answered
Joshua, 'Whatever you tell us, we will do; wherever you
17 send us, we will go. As we obeyed Moses, so will we
obey you; and may the LORD your God be with you as
18 he was with Moses! Whoever rebels against your authority, and fails to carry out all your orders, shall be put
to death. Only be strong and resolute.'

✳ This chapter is the prologue to the story of Israel's acquisition of her homeland. Specifically, it introduces chs. 2–12,
since it reports the preparations for the occupation of the
land; more generally, it introduces the entire book of Joshua,
since it anticipates all of Joshua's work and looks forward to
the time when Israel will be granted 'security' (verses 13, 15)
in her land. The first verse marks both a beginning and a
continuation. It is linked directly to Deut. 34, which reported

[*a*] *So Sept.; Heb. adds* and occupy it.

the death of Moses and Joshua's succession. With the death
of Moses, an era had come to an end. This new stage in
Israel's history begins with Joshua's assumption of leadership.

The chapter is a self-contained unit which stems in its
entirety from the pen of the Deuteronomistic historian (see
above, pp. 4–8). There is abundant evidence for this conclusion.
It is one of the passages which offers a comment on the narrative and unites the different elements. The Deuteronomistic
writers are fond of expressing themselves through second
person speeches such as the ones in this chapter. (Most of the
book of Deuteronomy consists. of second person speeches.)
The description of the promised land, and of the promise
itself (verses 3–4), parallels the vision and the style in Deut.
11: 24–5: 'Every place where you set the soles of your feet
shall be yours. Your borders shall run from the wilderness to
the Lebanon and from the River, the river Euphrates, to the
western sea. No man will be able to withstand you; the LORD
your God will put the fear and dread of you upon the whole
land on which you set foot, as he promised you.' As in
Deuteronomy, success depends upon strict obedience to the
law given by Moses. The 'book of the law' (verse 8) probably
refers to the law code in the central part of the book of
Deuteronomy itself. There are numerous verbal parallels to
the phraseology of that book: 'Be strong, be resolute...put
this people in possession of the land', in verse 6, parallels Deut.
3: 28. 'The LORD your God will grant you security here' in
verse 13 parallels Deut. 12: 10; 25: 19, etc. So this chapter is
a literary composition from the time of the Babylonian exile.

The words in this chapter concern Joshua and his generation,
but they are meant for the writer's own time. Though he
never mentions his audience explicitly, he is aware of them.
The past is not recounted here for its own sake, or out of an
antiquarian curiosity, but for the sake of the present and the
future. Each unit of this chapter is a sermon. Already the
historian is laying the foundation for an understanding of why
Israel succeeded where she succeeded and failed where she

failed. We can hear in these words an overtone of hope –
God is faithful to his promises and eager to grant Israel
security in her land – and also an undertone of threat – to the
extent that Israel is unfaithful she will fail. Those words
certainly had meaning for those who had experienced the
humiliation of the Babylonian exile and yet might begin to
think about a new occupation of the land or a re-establishment
of Israel in the promised land which she had lost.

This chapter consists of four parts, each one a different
speech. The parts are linked together by a very thin 'narrative'
framework (verses 1, 10, 12, 16*a*) which serves to introduce
each new address. No action or movement is reported. The
units are: The LORD's speech to Joshua (1–9), Joshua's speech to
the officers (10–11), Joshua's speech to the East Jordanian tribes
(12–15), and the reply of the East Jordanian tribes to Joshua
(16–18). These addresses consist of admonitions, instructions
and promises. We are not told where all this happened, but
are left to assume that Joshua and the tribes have not moved
from the place described in Deut. 34, the camp in 'the lowlands of Moab' (Deut. 34: 8).

1–9. In terms of style, tone and content, the LORD's speech
to Joshua has the appearance of a sermon. The LORD gives
Joshua the very general instructions 'to cross the Jordan, you
and this whole people of Israel' and to 'put this people in
possession of the land' but instructions are subordinated to
words of encouragement and promises. The means for accom-
plishing the goal are not given. Obedience to the law and
faithfulness to the LORD are more essential to success than is
strategy.

1. *Joshua son of Nun*: the name *Joshua* is formed, as are a
great many Israelite proper names, by combining a short form
of the name Yahweh with another word. It means 'Yahweh
is salvation', or perhaps 'may Yahweh save'. The names
'Hosea' and (through the Greek and Latin forms) 'Jesus' are
variations of the same name. *his assistant*: the same designation
is applied to Joshua in Exod. 24: 13; 33: 11 and Num. 11: 28

(N.E.B. 'who had served'). The term might also be translated 'minister', since it frequently refers to personal service or service in a religious ceremony, as for example that of the priests. The Old Testament preserves various traditions concerning Joshua's background, but always he appears as the assistant and then the successor of Moses. According to Exod. 17: 9, he was a leader in the battle against the Amalekites; later it appears he had been a young man in the service of Moses (Num. 11: 28). In Num. 13–14 he appears as one of the men sent by Moses to spy out the land of Canaan. Still later, his designation and ordination as the successor to Moses is reported (Num. 27: 15–23; cp. also Deut. 3: 21, 28).

2. *servant Moses*: the contrast between Moses as the servant of the LORD and Joshua as the assistant of Moses is striking. In Israelite tradition no figure compares with Moses. However, as this verse suggests, Moses stands at the head of a succession of leaders of Israel. Finally, at the end of his life, Joshua also is designated as 'servant of the LORD' (24: 29).

4. There are numerous descriptions in the Old Testament of the ideal boundaries of the promised land, but none is more comprehensive than this one. A simpler and doubtless older version is preserved in Gen. 15: 18: 'from the River of Egypt to the Great River, the river Euphrates'. The description before us seems to envisage three boundary points: *the desert* in the south and east, *the river Euphrates* in the north, and *the Great Sea* (the Mediterranean) in the west. The two other geographical terms present difficulties. *the Lebanon*, as a boundary point, is strange here, since this mountain range lies well inside the other boundary points. *across all the Hittite country* probably is a gloss, or late addition to the text, since it is not present in the Greek translation or in Deut. 11: 24, which otherwise parallels this verse. The phrase probably refers to territory in Syria, certainly not to the ancient kingdom of the Hittites in Asia Minor. At no time in her history were Israel's boundaries as wide as the ones described here. Only the empire of David almost reached these limits. The

boundaries actually describe a much larger territory than that divided among the tribes in chs. 13–19. So we have before us a somewhat vague outline of the ideal boundaries, one which draws upon several old Israelite traditions.

8. *This book of the law*: the previous verse has already pointed out that obedience to *the law* is the key to success. That point is emphasized once again, and it is made clear that the law of Moses is a written book. This particular formulation of the relationship between success and obedience to the written law is late, but it is rooted in the very old ideas of obedience to the terms of the covenant with the LORD.

10–11. After hearing the LORD's instructions, Joshua turns to *the officers* and instructs them to prepare the people to cross the Jordan and take the land. At this point there is no suggestion of warfare. In Deuteronomy, as here, *officers* is a general designation for civil and military leaders. Elsewhere the word equals 'elders', 'judges', and 'commanders'.

12–15. In the Deuteronomistic view of the conquest, the east Jordanian tribes (Reuben, Gad, and the half tribe of Manasseh) pose a special problem. They had already acquired their land before the crossing of the Jordan, but according to tradition all Israel was involved in the conquest of Canaan. The force of this speech, then, is to emphasize that point. On the settlement of the tribes in Transjordan see Num. 32; on the return of these tribes to their homeland, see ch. 22.

13, 15. *security*: the word often is translated 'rest', or 'peace' (cp. Deut. 25: 19; Judg. 3: 11, 30). *security* captures a meaning which is basic in the Deuteronomistic history of Israel. It does not refer so much to peace of mind or spiritual calm as to the external conditions of national security and peace which prevail when Israel is obedient to the law. The pattern which recurs in the book of Judges – rebellion against the Lord, oppression by enemies, repentance, the rise of a 'man to deliver them', then peace or security – makes this abundantly clear (cp. Judg. 3: 7–11). In 21: 43–5 'security' is the result of the fulfilment of the promise of the land. The

24

Letter to Hebrews has combined this idea of security with the divine rest on the seventh day into a new conception, one concerning the final age (cp. Heb. 4: 1–11).

16–18. This speech apparently is the response of the Trans-jordanian tribes to the instructions of Joshua, but its main purpose is to make it clear that the transfer of leadership has been accepted. The tribes will obey Joshua as they obeyed Moses. ✳

THE SPIES SENT TO JERICHO

Joshua son of Nun sent two spies out from Shittim 2 secretly with orders to reconnoitre the country. The two men came to Jericho and went to the house of a prostitute named Rahab, and spent the night there. It was reported 2 to the king of Jericho that some Israelites had arrived that night to explore the country. So the king sent to Rahab 3 and said, 'Bring out the men who have come to you and are now in your house; they are here to explore the whole country.' The woman, who had taken the two 4 men and hidden them,[a] replied, 'Yes, the men did come to me, but I did not know where they came from; and 5 when it was time to shut the gate at nightfall, they had gone. I do not know where they were going, but if you hurry after them, you will catch them up.' In fact, she 6 had taken them up on to the roof and concealed them among the stalks of flax which she had laid out there in rows. The messengers went in pursuit of them down the 7 road to the fords of the Jordan, and the gate was closed as soon as they had gone out. The men had not yet settled 8 down, when Rahab came up to them on the roof and 9 said to them, 'I know that the LORD has given this land

[a] *Prob. rdg.; Heb.* him.

to you, that terror of you has descended upon us all, and
that because of you the whole country is panic-stricken.
10 For we have heard how the LORD dried up the water of
the Red Sea[a] before you when you came out of Egypt,
and what you did to Sihon and Og, the two Amorite
11 kings beyond the Jordan, whom you put to death. When
we heard this, our courage failed us; your coming has
left no spirit in any of us; for the LORD your God is God
12 in heaven above and on earth below. Swear to me now
by the LORD that you will keep faith with my family, as
I have kept faith with you. Give me a token of good
13 faith; promise that you will spare the lives of my father
and mother, my brothers and sisters and all who belong
14 to them, and save us from death.' The men replied, 'Our
lives for yours, so long as you do not betray our business.
When the LORD gives us the country, we will deal
15 honestly and faithfully by you.' She then let them down
through an opening by a rope; for the house where she
16 lived was on an angle of the wall. 'Take to the hills,' she
said, 'or the pursuers will come upon you. Hide yourselves there for three days until they come back, and then
17 go on your way.' The men warned her that they would
18 be released from the oath she had made them take unless
she did what they told her. 'When we enter the land,'
they said, 'you must fasten this strand of scarlet cord in
the opening through which you have lowered us, and
get everybody together here in the house, your father and
19 mother, your brothers and all your family. If anybody
goes out of doors into the street, his blood shall be on his
own head; we shall be quit of the oath. But if a hand is

[a] *Or* the Sea of Reeds.

laid on anyone who stays indoors with you, his blood shall be on our heads. Remember too that, if you betray 20 our business, then we shall be quit of the oath you have made us take.' She replied, 'It shall be as you say', and 21 sent them away. They set off, and she fastened the strand of scarlet cord in the opening. The men made their way 22 into the hills and stayed there three days until the pursuers returned. They had searched all along the road, but had not found them.[a] The two men then turned and came 23 down from the hills, crossed the river and returned to Joshua son of Nun. They told him all that had happened to them and said to him, 'The LORD has put the whole 24 country into our hands, and now all its people are panic-stricken at our approach.'

✻ The story of the spies sent to Jericho has three main parts: the brief account of the sending of the spies and their arrival in Jericho (verse 1), the report of events in Jericho (verses 2–21), and the account of the escape and return of the spies to Joshua (verses 22–4). Most of the action in the body of the story (verses 2–21) occurs in three distinct scenes. First, there is the record of Rahab's efforts to hide the spies (verses 2–7). When the king of Jericho heard of the arrival of the enemy agents he sent men to Rahab's house, but she sent the men away and concealed the spies. Second, there is the report of an agreement between the prostitute and the spies. The scene is a conversation on the roof of her house (verses 8–14). In return for her help, the spies agreed to spare the lives of Rahab and her family when Israel conquered the land. Third, there is the account of an oath between Rahab and the spies, apparently as she is helping them escape through her window (verses 15–21). The agents once again promise to spare the

[a] three days...found them: *or* three days while the pursuers scoured the land and searched all along the road, but did not find them.

woman and her family if she remains faithful and follows
instructions. After the spies have made good their escape, the
story ends where it had begun, with the spies standing before
Joshua and giving their report that the people are 'panic-
stricken' (verse 24) at the approach of Israel.

Though the goal indicated at the beginning of the chapter
has been reached by its end, this chapter actually begins a
story that is not concluded until ch. 6. In general, chs. 2 and 6
together are the two parts of the account of the capture of the
city of Jericho. More specifically, the story of Rahab is not
concluded until 6: 17*b*, 22–5, which reports how Israel spared
the prostitute and her family, as the spies had promised.

The general thread of the story begun in ch. 1 is continued
to the extent that it deals with preparations for the entrance
into the promised land. However, these preparations are quite
different from those in ch. 1, and a number of factors indicate
a rather clear break between the two chapters. The style
changes dramatically; except in isolated instances the Deuteronomistic prose, such as we saw in ch. 1, is missing here. The
location of the Israelite camp is described differently: *Shittim*
(verse 1) had not been mentioned in the Deuteronomistic
version of Israel's travels in the wilderness. Furthermore,
ch. 1 seems to lead more directly to the crossing of the Jordan;
that is, ch. 3 is a more logical continuation than is ch. 2.
Finally, the reference to a crossing 'within three days' in 1: 11
accommodates *either* the events in ch. 2 (cp. verse 22) *or* those
at the beginning of ch. 3 (cp. verse 2), but not both.

These factors suggest that this chapter contains the first of
the older stories which the Deuteronomistic historian used
in writing his history of the conquest. An examination of the
style of the chapter confirms the conclusion. The editor
apparently allowed the older story to stand very much as he
received it. (For his additions see below.) So the story of
Rahab and the Israelite spies probably had been written down
long before the time of the Deuteronomistic historian. Furthermore, there are indications that the story once circulated

as oral tradition. There are several inconsistencies, repetitions, and changes in the style which probably resulted from the oral transmission of the story, and also from the combination of more than one version of what happened. Thus, the sequence of events is somewhat confusing. The spies were sent out to reconnoitre the country and they returned with a report concerning 'the whole country' (verse 24), but the story itself speaks only of their activities in Jericho. The order of events in the first scene is especially confusing, since there are two reports that Rahab hid the spies (verses 4*a* and 6), both of which disrupt the story. This difficulty is obscured somewhat in the N.E.B. (as in most other translations) by translating the Hebrew in the pluperfect: 'had taken the two men and hidden them', and 'she had taken them up on to the roof and concealed them'.

Similar problems arise in the story framework of the third scene (verses 15–21). As the story stands, we read that Rahab let the spies down on a rope through her window, gave them instructions for their escape, they then responded with an extended speech, and she finally sent them on their way. We are left with the picture of the spies pausing to complete their agreement with the prostitute as they cling to a rope from her window. Moreover, we would have expected the men to state the terms of their agreement before they actually agreed to Rahab's request for an oath between them (verses 12–14).

In its present literary context, the story of Rahab and the spies must be viewed as an aetiological story. That is to say, in view of its present conclusion in ch. 6 its aim (or at least one of its central aims) is to account for something by giving the story of its origin. The story explains why and how the family or clan of Rahab was allowed to live in Israel. However, it is no longer possible to say with certainty whether or not the story *originated* as an aetiology. The most obvious sign of the aetiology, the formula in 6: 25, probably was not part of the original story. It stems from the redactor who combined the story of Rahab with the story of the destruction of Jericho. On the other hand, the aetiological features are not limited to this conclusion: ch. 2 as a whole seems to anticipate such an ending. Thus various suggestions concerning the original shape of the story have been presented. Some have suggested that the story originally explained the presence of prostitutes connected with religious ceremonies in Israel in general or in Jericho in particular. Others have argued that the story of Rahab once told a story of the capture of Jericho different from the one in ch. 6. According to this interpretation, while ch. 6 reports the capture of the city by an act of God, ch. 2 once reported how the city was taken with the help of an act of treason by Rahab.

However the story appeared when it was being circulated orally, one of its main purposes in its final form is to explain how the family of Rahab survived the conquest. The story, however, has other purposes as well. The two main themes are (1) the mission of the spies, presented in the beginning and concluding sections of the chapter, and (2) Rahab's actions on behalf of the spies and Israel's response (reported in 6: 22–5). The tale of the spies serves a significant role in the narrative of the conquest as a whole. The point of this story is clear in the results of the expedition. It is not intended to show Joshua's cunning or military skill. The only information which the spies gathered was the intelligence that the inhabitants of the land stand in terror before Israel: 'The LORD has put the whole country into our hands' (verse 24). This formula is used over and over in the accounts of Israel's holy wars. Such a war cannot begin without the assurance that the LORD is with the people to give them victory. Given the idea of the holy war, the spy story is placed here to show that the conquest did not begin until the will of the LORD had been determined.

1. *two spies*: there are several other reports of the sending of spies into the promised land ahead of the invading Israelites. Joshua himself had been one of the twelve spies (one from

each tribe) sent by Moses to report on the land and on the strength of the enemy (Num. 13; cp. also Deut. 1: 22ff.). That expedition from the southern wilderness into southern Palestine resulted in the decision not to enter the promised land from the south. Moses also sent spies to Jazer, a city in Transjordan (Num. 21: 32). Joshua sent spies ahead of Israel to the city of Ai (7: 2ff.), and the tribe of Dan sent five spies to locate a territory where they could move (Judg. 18: 2ff.). The mission of these particular spies is not specified in detail. They are simply *to reconnoitre the country*.

Shittim: the site of Israel's camp in Transjordan (see Map 1) is probably to be identified with the 'Abel-shittim' of Num. 33: 49 (cp. also Num. 25: 1). In the fuller description of the location, Abel-shittim is mentioned as one of the boundaries of the camp 'in the lowlands of Moab by the Jordan near Jericho'. The place has been identified variously with Tell el-Kefrein, about 11 kilometres (7 miles) east of the Jordan, almost 10 kilometres (6 miles) north of the Dead Sea, and Tell el-Hammām, 3 kilometres (less than 2 miles) east of the former site. The name is mentioned here simply to specify the region of Israel's camp across the Jordan from Jericho.

Jericho: the ancient city was located at Tell es-Sulṭān, just north of the Jericho of New Testament times. The site is deep in the Jordan valley, approximately 11 kilometres (7 miles) north of the Dead Sea, see Map 1. From their camp in the lowlands of Moab the Israelites approached the nearest city in Palestine proper.

prostitute: some have suggested that Rahab was a cultic prostitute, and that this story once explained the existence of Canaanite cultic prostitution within Israel. But while it is true that some ceremonies of ancient Near Eastern religions included temple prostitutes, the evidence for such a conclusion is lacking. The Hebrew term translated here (*zonah*) may refer to either secular or cultic prostitution. The specific term for a cultic prostitute (*qedeshah*) does not appear.

2–7. The point of this unit is to describe Rahab's first two acts on behalf of the Israelite spies. She deceived the king's representatives into thinking that the spies had already gone and hid the spies on the roof of her house under flax which had been placed there to dry. Her reasons for doing so become apparent only in the next scene.

2. *the king of Jericho*: the heads of the Canaanite cities which Joshua opposed usually are designated as 'kings' (cp. 5: 1; 8: 1ff.; 9: 1ff.). Actually they were the rulers of the numerous little city states in Palestine.

8–14. Rahab declares to the spies that the LORD has given the land to Israel (verse 9). She confesses her faith in the LORD and asks for a sworn agreement that *you will keep faith with my family, as I have kept faith with you* (verse 12). This agreement can only be a covenant, since covenants ordinarily are sealed with an oath. Rahab's recital of the history of Israel depends heavily on the language and style of Deuteronomy. Verses 9 *b*, 10 *b*, 11 *b*, and 24 *b* stem from the Deuteronomistic historian.

15–21. This section reports Rahab's third step on behalf of the spies, her assistance in their escape, and further details of the agreement. Her house apparently was built against the wall of the city, since she could let them escape on a rope through her window. The *strand of scarlet cord in the opening* (verse 18) is simply a sign by which the Israelites will recognize the prostitute's house and spare its inhabitants. ✶

ISRAEL CROSSES THE JORDAN

3 Joshua rose early in the morning, and he and all the Israelites set out from Shittim and came to the Jordan,
2 where they encamped before crossing the river. At the end of three days the officers passed through the camp,
3 and gave this order to the people: 'When you see the Ark of the Covenant of the LORD your God being carried forward by the levitical priests, then you too shall leave

your positions and set out. Follow it, but do not go close 4
to it; keep some distance behind, about a thousand yards.[a]
This will show you the way you are to go, for you have
not travelled this way before.' Joshua then said to the 5
people, 'Hallow yourselves, for tomorrow the LORD will
do a great miracle among you.' To the priests he said, 6
'Lift up the Ark of the Covenant and pass in front of the
people.' So they lifted up the Ark of the Covenant and
went in front of the people. Then the LORD said to Joshua, 7
'Today I will begin to make you stand high in the eyes of
all Israel, and they shall know that I will be with you as
I was with Moses. Give orders to the priests who carry 8
the Ark of the Covenant, and tell them that when they
come to the edge of the waters of the Jordan, they are to
take their stand in the river.'

Then Joshua said to the Israelites, 'Come here and 9
listen to the words of the LORD your God. By this you 10
shall know that the living God is among you and that he
will drive out before you the Canaanites, the Hittites, the
Hivites, the Perizzites, the Girgashites, the Amorites, and
the Jebusites: the Ark of the Covenant of the LORD,[b] 11
the lord of all the earth, is to cross the Jordan at your head.
Choose twelve men from the tribes of Israel, one man 12
from each tribe. When the priests carrying the Ark of the 13
LORD, the lord of all the earth, set foot in the waters of the
Jordan, then the waters of the Jordan will be cut off; the
water coming down from upstream will stand piled up
like a bank.' So the people set out from their tents to 14
cross the Jordan, with the priests in front of them carrying

[a] *Lit.* two thousand cubits.
[b] of the LORD: *prob. rdg., cp. verse 17; Heb. om.*

15 the Ark of the Covenant. Now the Jordan is in full flood
in all its reaches throughout the time of harvest. When
the priests reached the Jordan and dipped their feet in the
16 water at the edge, the water coming down from upstream was brought to a standstill; it piled up like a bank
for a long way back, as far as Adam, a town near Zarethan.
The waters coming down to the Sea of the Arabah, the
Dead Sea, were completely cut off, and the people crossed
17 over opposite Jericho. The priests carrying the Ark of the
Covenant of the LORD stood firm on the dry bed in the
middle of the Jordan; and all Israel passed over on dry
ground until the whole nation had crossed the river.

* The main purpose of this chapter and the one which follows
is to report how Israel actually entered Palestine itself by
means of a miraculous crossing of the river Jordan. The two
chapters form a single, though very complex, unit. Because of
its importance to ancient Israel, the theme of the river crossing
must have been recounted often in stories and songs, many
of which were used in worship (cp. Ps. 114). The complexity
of the account before us reflects its use over many centuries.

The first part of the story of the crossing (ch. 3) consists of
two main sections, the account of the preparations (3: 1–13)
and the report of the miracle at the river (3: 14–17). The
preparations included the journey from Shittim to a new
encampment near the Jordan and a series of speeches giving
instructions for the crossing. The speeches are linked together
by a thin narrative thread. The report of the crossing con-
centrates on the miracle of the waters; once the people have
been prepared properly and the miracle has occurred, the
crossing itself is a simple matter.

The chapter has been edited by the Deuteronomistic historian. His additions to the old story are found in 3: 2–4,
6–10, 17*b*. One purpose of these additions is to emphasize the

34

importance of obedience to the LORD's instructions and another was to stress that the native inhabitants of the land are being driven out by Israel's God. The editor also continues to elevate Joshua as the legitimate successor to Moses (cp. 1: 5, 17).

There must have been many older stories about the entrance into the land. Parts of at least two different traditions have been preserved here. Most of the evidence for the presence of two traditions is found in the second part of the account (ch. 4); here we should only notice that 'twelve men' were chosen (3: 12) and then 'the priests' carried the Ark (3: 13).

The account as it now stands presents the crossing as a liturgical event, that is, an act of worship. The 'Ark of the Covenant' is carried before the people by the 'levitical priests' (3: 3), ritual preparations must be made ('Hallow yourselves', 3: 5), and the people set out in solemn procession. As the story continues further similarities to a service of worship are evident. It seems likely, therefore, that the story was used in a liturgy, perhaps at a sanctuary in nearby Gilgal. The story would have provided the framework for a re-enactment of the original crossing.

In this story the parallels between the careers of Moses and Joshua become more and more obvious. The liturgical elements of the crossing are similar in many ways to the ritual preparations for the appearance of the LORD on Mount Sinai (Exod. 19). Both leaders had sent spies ahead of them. More basic are the similarities between the account of the miraculous crossing of the sea (Exod. 14–15) and the crossing of the river Jordan. The place of the pillar of cloud and fire at the head of the procession in the time of Moses is taken here by the Ark. Both miracles are closely associated with the celebration of the Passover (Exod. 12: 1 – 13: 16; Josh. 5: 10–12).

1. On the location of *Shittim*, see the note to 2: 1.

3. *the Ark* was one of Israel's more ancient and most important religious institutions. Though there are many old traditions concerning this portable shrine, the only full descriptions

of it are too late to be reliable. The Priestly writer (cp. especially Exod. 25: 10–22) describes it as a box overlaid with gold, gives its precise measurements and a description of its decorations. In all the traditions the Ark symbolizes the presence of the LORD, and perhaps once was understood as a throne for his invisible presence. In the older stories, as in this account, the Ark often leads Israel into battle. It obviously was a rallying point for the Israelite tribes for both worship and war (cp. 1 Sam. 4). In some traditions the Ark is understood as a container for other religious objects; thus in 4: 16 there is a reference to 'the Tokens' which is a term used to refer to the tablets on which the law was inscribed (cp. Exod. 25: 16; 32: 15). It is significant that both the old traditions and the Deuteronomistic editor have associated the Ark with a religious ceremony and with the number twelve for the Israelite tribes. These associations strongly suggest that the Ark was one of the oldest symbols of the tribes even before they became a nation, and that it was a basic part of tribal worship. Other stories of the Ark (cp. especially 1 Sam. 4–7; 2 Sam. 6) suggest that it may have been moved from one sanctuary to another.

This is the only point where those who carried the Ark across the Jordan are identified as *levitical priests*. The phrase (literally 'the priests, the Levites') is common to the book of Deuteronomy. It refers to the priestly family that descended from the patriarch Levi. It certainly was an early and important priesthood, which often is associated with the Ark. As time goes on, especially following the centralization of worship in Jerusalem, this hereditary priesthood becomes less important, to the point that in the post-exilic period they have become a subordinate group among the priests of the second temple.

4. *a thousand yards*: literally, 'two thousand cubits'. It was believed to be dangerous for ordinary people to approach holy things too closely. According to 2 Sam. 6: 1–11, when David attempted to move the Ark the oxen pulling the cart

stumbled, and when Uzzah tried to prevent the Ark from falling he touched it and was struck dead.

5. *Hallow yourselves*: sanctification, through one means or another, was required before participation in worship or in the holy war. Here Israel is told to be ritually clean because of the miracle which the LORD is about to do. Such sanctification included abstinence from sexual activity and certain foods, and rites of purification, such as ritual washing (cp. Exod. 19: 10–14; Num. 11: 18). The word translated here *great miracle* refers to a wonderful or awesome event by which the LORD makes his power visible.

7. The parallel between Moses and Joshua becomes explicit. According to this note, the purpose of the miracle is to make it clear to the people that the LORD is active through Joshua as he was through Moses.

10. The reference to the LORD as *the living God* (or 'a living God') may be a way of contrasting the God of Israel with the dying and rising fertility gods of her neighbours.

Lists of the peoples whom the LORD will *drive out* of the land are not infrequent. There are five similar lists in the book of Joshua. The lists give six or, as here, seven peoples. (The *Girgashites* are mentioned in only a few of the lists.) These tables reflect the very complex ethnic situation in Palestine before – and even after – the Israelites entered the land. All the names, with the possible exception of the *Perizzites*, refer to ethnic groups, most of which are known from non-biblical sources. In the Old Testament, *Canaanites* often is a general designation for all the pre-Israelite population of the land. The territory which Israel occupied is frequently called the land of Canaan (cp. 7: 9; Gen. 12: 5–6). This list and other references know the Canaanites as just one group among many. Likewise the *Amorites* are known as the pre-Israelite population in general (Gen. 15: 16; Amos 2: 9) and as one group among several (Deut. 1: 19; Josh. 10: 5ff.). The Old Testament designates a number of individuals as *Hittites*, most frequently associating them with the south (Gen. 23: 10).

The term *Hivites* probably is an Israelite corruption of the term Hurrians (called 'Horites' in the Old Testament). The *Jebusites* are identified as the clan which controlled the city of Jerusalem (2 Sam. 5: 6–7). The *Perizzites* and the *Girgashites* are mentioned only in lists, hence nothing is known about who they were or where they lived.

11. The N.E.B. has emended the text to conform to verses 3 and 17. The Hebrew reads literally: 'Behold the Ark of the Covenant of the Lord of all the earth.'

13. Now the nature of the miracle becomes clear: when the Ark reaches the Jordan the river will be *cut off* so that the Israelites may cross. It is not unusual for Old Testament story-tellers to repeat themselves, that is, to tell what will happen and then to describe what happened (verses 15–17).

15. It was necessary for the narrator to point out that it was *the time of harvest* when the river was *in full flood* from the melting of the snow on Mount Hermon. Otherwise no miracle would be required since the Jordan can be forded easily most of the year. In fact, the Old Testament frequently reports how individuals and even large groups crossed the Jordan without difficulty (cp. Judg. 3: 28; 8: 4; 1 Sam. 13: 7; 2 Sam. 17: 24).

16. The text presents the picture of an invisible dam, with the waters backing up behind it like a lake. Some commentators have attempted to account for this event by referring to records of natural blockage of the Jordan because of landslides or earthquakes. Such explanations fail to account for the very convenient timing of this blockage, or – more important – for the character of the story itself, in which the miraculous nature of the event is emphasized. The account is theology, not history. The story is intended to show how the LORD's awesome power was active through the Ark and his chosen leader, Joshua. *

THE COMPLETION OF THE CROSSING AND THE ERECTION OF MEMORIAL STONES

When the whole nation had finished crossing the **4** Jordan, the LORD said to Joshua, 'Take twelve men from **2** the people, one from each tribe, and order them to lift **3** up twelve stones from this place, out of the middle of the Jordan, where the feet of the priests stood firm. They are to carry them across and set them down in the camp where you spend the night.' Joshua summoned the twelve **4** men whom he had chosen out of the Israelites, one man from each tribe, and said to them, 'Cross over in front **5** of the Ark of the LORD your God as far as the middle of the Jordan, and let each of you take a stone and hoist it on his shoulder, one for each of the tribes of Israel. These **6** stones are to stand as a memorial among you; and in days to come, when your children ask you what these stones mean, you shall tell them how the waters of the Jordan **7** were cut off before the Ark of the Covenant of the LORD when it crossed the Jordan.[a] Thus these stones will always be a reminder to the Israelites.' The Israelites did as **8** Joshua had commanded: they lifted up twelve stones from the middle of the Jordan, as the LORD had instructed Joshua, one for each of the tribes of Israel, carried them across to the camp and set them down there.

Joshua set up twelve stones in the middle of the Jordan **9** at the place where the priests stood who carried the Ark of the Covenant, and there they are to this day. The **10** priests carrying the Ark remained standing in the middle of the Jordan until every command which the LORD had

[a] *So Sept.; Heb. adds* the waters of the Jordan were cut off.

told Joshua to give to the people was fulfilled,[a] and the
11 people had made good speed across. When all the people
had finished crossing, then the Ark of the LORD crossed,
12 and the priests with it.[b] At the head of the Israelites, there
crossed over the Reubenites, the Gadites, and the half
tribe of Manasseh, as a fighting force, as Moses had told
13 them to do; about forty thousand strong, drafted for
active service, they crossed over to the lowlands of
Jericho in the presence of the LORD to do battle.

14   That day the LORD made Joshua stand very high in the
eyes of all Israel, and the people revered him, as they had
revered Moses all his life.

15, 16   The LORD said to Joshua, 'Command the priests carrying the Ark of the Tokens to come up from the Jordan.'
17 So Joshua commanded the priests to come up from the
18 Jordan; and when the priests carrying the Ark of the
Covenant of the LORD came up from the river-bed, they
had no sooner set foot on dry land than the waters of the
Jordan came back to their place and filled up all its
19 reaches as before. On the tenth day of the first month the
people came up out of the Jordan and camped in Gilgal
20 in the district east of Jericho, and there Joshua set up the
twelve stones which they had taken from the Jordan.
21 He said to the Israelites, 'In days to come, when your
22 descendants ask their fathers what these stones mean, you
shall explain that the Jordan was dry when Israel crossed
23 over, and that the LORD your God dried up the waters of
the Jordan in front of you until you had gone across, just
as the LORD your God did at the Red Sea when he dried

[a] *So Sept.; Heb. adds* according to all that Moses commanded Joshua.
[b] *Prob. rdg.; Heb. adds* before the people.

it up for us until we had crossed. Thus all people on earth 24
will know how strong is the hand of the LORD; and thus
they will stand in awe of the LORD your God for ever.'

When all the Amorite kings to the west of the Jordan 5
and all the Canaanite kings by the sea-coast heard that
the LORD had dried up the waters before the advance of
the Israelites until they had crossed, their courage melted
away and there was no more spirit left in them for fear
of the Israelites.

✻ The story of the crossing of the Jordan is continued and
completed. The first part of the account (ch. 3) has emphasized the preparations. The second part stresses the results of
the miraculous event, that is, the building of the memorial
and the effect of the miracle upon Israel and upon her enemies.
The brief report of the crossing itself (3: 17) links the two
parts.

The dominant theme of this chapter is the commemoration
of Israel's entrance into Palestine. The first unit (4: 1–8) reports
how stones were taken from the middle of the Jordan in order
to construct a monument in *the camp* (verse 8). The second
unit (9–13) reports the erection of twelve stones as a monument in the *middle of the Jordan* and the completion of the
crossing by the people and the priests. The next paragraph
(14) reports how Joshua is respected as Moses had been. The
fourth unit (15–24) reports (once again) that the priests came
out of the Jordan, that the waters then returned, that the people
established a camp in *Gilgal* and *there Joshua set up the twelve
stones which they had taken from the Jordan*. The final section
(5: 1) summarizes the effect of the news about Israel's advance
upon the rulers of the country: *their courage melted away*.

Any attempt to outline or to summarize the story reveals
inconsistencies and repetitions which must have resulted from
the combination of several traditions and the work of more
than one writer. We are hard pressed to state precisely what

is supposed to have happened, or to list without contradiction the sequence of events. Where, for example, were the twelve stones set up? According to verse 9 they were erected *in the middle of the Jordan*, but according to verses 8 and 19–20 they were set up *in Gilgal*. Further, there are two slightly different explanations of the purpose of the stones, one in 4: 6–8 and another in 4: 21–4. Twice instructions are given to choose twelve men (3: 12 and 4: 2). The sequence of events is unclear, especially since there are three references (3: 17; 4: 1; 4: 10) to the completion of the crossing.

Some of the difficulties can be solved when one recognizes that the Deuteronomistic editor has been at work, and his additions have produced some repetitions. His distinctive style and particular concerns are seen in the explanation of the meaning of the event for future generations (4: 6–7, 21–4), the special interest in the part played by the Transjordanian tribes (4: 12–13), the emphasis upon the respect for Joshua as the rightful successor to Moses (4: 14), and the report of the awe inspired by the LORD's action (4: 24 – 5: 1).

However, when one examines the material which remains, it is safe to conclude that there were originally at least two different stories, one which spoke of a monument at the old sanctuary of Gilgal, and another which placed the monument in the middle of the Jordan. In addition, there may have been another tradition which stressed the role of the Ark. It is not possible to reconstruct any complete story, since the traditions have been combined in such a way that no single tradition remains intact. But we can see that Israel reflected upon the entrance of her ancestors into the promised land in many different ways.

The liturgical character of the account, already noted in ch. 3, is continued. The Ark, the priests, and the processional character of the crossing suggest a ritual. Furthermore, Gilgal, where the tribes encamped, was one of Israel's earliest places of worship.

2. The choice of *twelve men* is significant. The number was

not magical in ancient Israel, but simply designated the number of the tribes. Other non-Israelite twelve- and six-tribe
groups are mentioned in the Old Testament. This suggests
that the traditions here arose before the monarchy was established, that is, in the tribal era.

6–7. According to this writer, the stones are to serve as
a memorial and *a reminder*, that is, they are to keep alive the
memory of the crossing. When future generations ask about
the meaning of the monument, the story will be told again.
Thus later Israelites will know of the LORD's mighty act.

The *Ark* is designated in various ways. Here, as in 4: 18, it
is called the *Ark of the Covenant of the LORD*. The *Covenant*
was the solemn agreement between the LORD and Israel, in
which he became their God and they his people. For the
description of an ancient Israelite covenant ceremony, cp.
ch. 24.

9. The phrase *to this day* is a common formula for concluding aetiological stories, that is, stories which explain some
phenomenon –. such as the monument mentioned here – by
giving an account of its origin. The tradition here has in
mind a monument *in the middle of the Jordan*, which might or
might not have been visible.

12. *the Reubenites, the Gadites, and the half tribe of Manasseh*
are the tribes who had already acquired their land east of the
Jordan. When these tribes asked for land east of the Jordan
(Num. 32), Moses granted their request on the condition that
they help the other tribes to acquire their land west of the
river. The note here (cp. also Deut. 3: 18–20 and Josh. 1:
13–15) is added in order to point out that all twelve Israelite
tribes took part in the conquest.

16. *the Tokens*: the tablets of the law (cp. the note on 3: 3).

19. *the tenth day of the first month*: the date is given exactly
in order to conform to the time of the Passover, the celebration of which is reported in the next chapter (5: 10ff.). *the
first month* was Abib, or, later, Nisan, the Babylonian name.
The date is consistent with 'the time of harvest' (3: 15) in

March–April. This precise dating immediately before the time of Passover lends support to the idea that a ritual is being described.

Gilgal is located quite generally *east of Jericho*. The location figures prominently in the story of the conquest as the base of military operations. The word is taken to mean 'circle of stones', and thus easily is associated with the twelve-stone monument. It is known that Gilgal was one of Israel's early sanctuaries, and that the Ark apparently was located there during some periods. The place was denounced as a place of false worship by some of the early prophets (cp. Amos 4: 4; 5: 5; Hos. 4: 15; 9: 15; 12: 11). Concerning the location of Gilgal, see Map 1 and the Gazetteer.

23. *Red Sea*: the N.E.B. here follows the earliest translations instead of the Hebrew text, in which the phrase means literally 'the Sea of Reeds'. The basic account of the crossing of the sea is found in Exod. 14–15.

24. The meaning and results of the miracle at the Jordan are explained. According to this writer, the event was not just an unusual event, nor simply for the purpose of providing Israel with easy access to the promised land. It was the LORD's means of showing that he was indeed God.

5: 1. Now the results of the crossing are described more specifically. The Amorite and Canaanite *kings* – that is, rulers of the Palestinian city states – stand in awe and terror of Israel's God and of Israel herself. The results of the forthcoming war have already been determined. ✳

CIRCUMCISION AT GILGAL

2 At that time the LORD said to Joshua, 'Make knives of flint, seat yourself, and make Israel a circumcised people 3 again.' Joshua thereupon made knives of flint and circum- 4 cised the Israelites at Gibeath-haaraloth.*ᵃ* This is why

[a] *That is* the Hill of Foreskins.

Joshua circumcised them: all the males who came out of Egypt, all the fighting men, had died in the wilderness on the journey from Egypt. The people who came out of 5 Egypt had all been circumcised, but not those who had been born in the wilderness during the journey. For the 6 Israelites travelled in the wilderness for forty years, until the whole nation, all the fighting men among them, had passed away, all who came out of Egypt and had dis-obeyed the voice of the LORD. The LORD swore that he would not allow any of these to see the land which he had sworn to their fathers to give us, a land flowing with milk and honey. So it was their sons, whom he had raised 7 up in their place, that Joshua circumcised; they were uncircumcised because they had not been circumcised on the journey. When the circumcision of the whole nation 8 was complete, they stayed where they were in camp until they had recovered. The LORD then said to Joshua, 'Today 9 I have rolled away from you the reproaches of the Egyptians.' Therefore the place is called Gilgal[a] to this very day.

✳ Joshua's first duty upon arriving in the land of Palestine was to circumcise the Israelites. The report of the ceremony is the first of three little stories of events which happened at Gilgal before the actual wars of conquest began. The others are the Passover (5: 10–11) and Joshua's encounter with the captain of the army of the LORD (5: 13–15). The account of the circumcision occurs at this point in the narrative because of the regulations concerning the celebration of Passover. According to Exod. 12: 43–9, one had to be circumcised to participate in the ceremony. The entire sequence of events as Israel enters the land is liturgical. The people are preparing

[a] *That is* Rolling Stones.

45

themselves for a holy war, one which is more religious than military.

The account of the circumcision consists of two parts, a short, terse narrative (verses 2–3, 8–9) and a verbose explanation (verses 4–7). These two parts correspond to the literary history of the material. The story itself is one of the ancient traditions which had come to be associated with the region of Gilgal; the explanation was added by the Deuteronomistic editor. As the old story now stands, it is an aetiological tale; that is, it gives a narrative account of how the name Gilgal originated (verse 9). In his addition (verses 4–7), the editor stands outside the story and comments upon it. His purpose is not only to explain why the ceremony was necessary, but also – in his comment on disobedience and its punishment – to draw a lesson from the past.

2. The reference to *knives of flint* (see also Exod. 4: 24–6) indicates both the antiquity and the religious character of circumcision. By the time of Joshua, flint tools had been replaced by metal instruments except for such special occasions as the one described here (cp. also Exod. 20: 25). According to the Priestly writer (Gen. 17: 10–14), the rite of circumcision originated in the time of Abraham as a sign of membership in the covenant community. The instructions to circumcise the people *again* assumes that all the original generation of the exodus had died, except Joshua and perhaps Caleb (see verses 5–6 and Num. 14: 30ff.), and that circumcision had not been performed during the wilderness period. However, the latter assumption is contrary to the usual practice in historical times of circumcising infant males on the eighth day (Lev. 12: 1–3).

3. *Gibeath-haaraloth*: the conclusion of the story (verse 9) implies that Gilgal once was called 'Hill of Foreskins'. However, it is possible that our story originally did not refer to Gilgal at all, but rather was an aetiology of the name, 'Hill of Foreskins'.

9. The explanation of the name *Gilgal* is a popular ety-

mology; that is, it is not a scientifically correct explanation of the word, but one based on the similarity of the name to the verb *rolled away* (*gālal*). Gilgal probably originally meant 'a circle (of stones)', or 'rolling stones' (cp. 4: 20).

Since *the reproaches of the Egyptians* are not specified, one can only speculate concerning the intended reference. Whether they refer to the hardships of the Egyptian slavery, the fact that Israel lived among foreigners or to some very specific religious offence, is not clear. Whatever they were, *the reproaches* now have been removed from the covenant people. ✻

THE FIRST PASSOVER IN PALESTINE

The Israelites encamped in Gilgal, and at sunset on the 10 fourteenth day of the month they kept the Passover in the lowlands of Jericho. On the day after the Passover, 11 they ate their unleavened cakes and parched grain, and that day it was the produce of the country. It was from 12 that day, when they first ate the produce of the country, that the manna ceased. The Israelites received no more manna; and that year they ate what had grown in the land of Canaan.

✻ After Joshua had circumcised the Israelites the people could properly celebrate the festival of Passover. This little account of the first Passover in Canaan appears to be a relatively ancient tradition, though the dates in verses 10 and 11 may be later additions. The story does not describe the celebration; it simply reports that it happened and when and where. Though the account is brief, the event which it reports was a turning-point of great significance for Israel. The period of the wilderness wandering now formally comes to a close. It ended as it had begun, with the celebration of Passover. The manna ceases; according to Exod. 16: 35, it had sustained the people for forty years.

In addition to taking note of the end of an era, this report advances the idea of the conquest of Canaan as a holy war. The covenant people, obedient to the law (see the note on 1: 8), in this case the law concerning Passover, have been granted the land. They now have only to remain obedient and take possession of it.

10. The establishment of the camp in Gilgal had already been reported in 4: 19. According to Exod. 12: 1-6, the *fourteenth day* of the first month (cp. 4: 19) was the day in the ritual calendar set aside for Passover. *Passover* was the festival which commemorated Israel's exodus from Egypt. The first celebration was said to have occurred on the night when the first-born of the Egyptians were killed and the Israelites allowed to depart from Egypt (Exod. 12). It was a feast involving the ritual killing and eating of a lamb or a kid by each Israelite family. The ceremony probably stems from the practices of bedouin shepherds which are much earlier than the exodus.

11. The mention of *unleavened cakes* is an allusion to the feast of Unleavened Bread. By historical times in Israel, Passover and Unleavened Bread had become one ceremony. While they are said to have been instituted at the same time, it seems most likely that originally they were two separate and distinct festivals. Often one is mentioned without reference to the other, and each suggests a different background. While Passover probably originated as a one-night feast among wandering herdsmen, Unleavened Bread was a seven-day celebration which fits the agricultural calendar of settled farmers. It is therefore unlikely that the Israelites participated in the feast of Unleavened Bread before their arrival in Palestine.

12. The *manna* was the food miraculously provided by the LORD in the wilderness in response to the Israelites' complaints (see Exod. 16). The gift is explained and described variously. One writer (the Yahwist; see *The Making of the Old Testament* in this series, pp. 60ff.) speaks of it as 'bread from heaven'

48

and describes it as 'white, like coriander seed, and it tasted like a wafer made with honey' (Exod. 16: 4, 31). The Priestly writer describes it as related to the dew, 'fine as hoar-frost on the ground' (Exod. 16: 14). In Deuteronomy, the gift is explained as a lesson: 'He humbled you and made you hungry; then he fed you on manna which neither you nor your fathers had known before, to teach you that man cannot live on bread alone but lives by every word that comes from the mouth of the LORD' (Deut. 8: 3). When it was no longer needed, the manna ceased as miraculously as it had begun. ✹

JOSHUA AND THE CAPTAIN OF THE LORD'S ARMY

When Joshua came near Jericho he looked up and saw 13 a man standing in front of him with a drawn sword in his hand. Joshua went up to him and said, 'Are you for us or for our enemies?' And the man said to him, 'I[a] am 14 here as captain of the army of the LORD.' Joshua fell down before him, face to the ground, and said, 'What have you to say to your servant, my lord?' The captain of the 15 LORD's army said to him, 'Take off your sandals; the place where you are standing is holy'; and Joshua did so.

✹ This mysterious encounter was the last event before the actual wars of conquest began. Joshua met a man whom he mistook for an ordinary soldier but discovered to be an emissary of the LORD. After a brief dialogue, the encounter ends suddenly and inconclusively. It is reasonable to suppose that part of the original story is missing. Stories which begin as this one does are frequently explanations of the holiness of a particular place. Thus David, after seeing the avenging angel of the LORD, bought the spot and built an altar there (2 Sam. 24: 16-25). Gen. 28: 10-22 similarly explains the establishment of the altar at Bethel. Another possibility is that the

[a] *So some MSS.; others* And the man said, 'No, I...

tradition once reported the vocation of Joshua. This interpretation is suggested by the close parallels to the report of
the call of Moses. Verse 15 is an exact quotation of Exod. 3: 5.
In its abbreviated form in the present context, the story
advances two themes which were important both in the old
traditions and the Deuteronomistic history. First, Joshua is
elevated and his life shown to parallel that of his predecessor.
Second, final divine sanction and leadership are provided for
the war of conquest.

13. *near Jericho*: literally, 'in' or 'at' Jericho.

a man: the encounter with a man which turns out to be a
meeting with God or his messengers is not uncommon in the
Old Testament; see Gen. 18; 32: 22–32.

14. *captain of the army of the LORD*: the man answers
Joshua's question literally, 'No, for I have come as captain of
the host of the LORD.' *army of the LORD* is a reasonable
interpretation in the context. The 'host' may refer to the
angels, the heavenly bodies (cp. Judg. 5: 20) or to Israel's
army. The term is common in reports of holy wars. ✶

THE CONQUEST OF JERICHO

6 Jericho was bolted and barred against the Israelites;
2 no one went out, no one came in. The LORD said to
Joshua, 'Look, I have delivered Jericho and her king[a]
3 into your hands. You shall march round the city with all
your fighting men, making the circuit of it once, for six
4 days running. Seven priests shall go in front of the Ark
carrying seven trumpets made from rams' horns. On
the seventh day you shall march round the city seven
5 times and the priests shall blow their trumpets. At the
blast of the rams' horns, when you hear the trumpet
sound, the whole army shall raise a great shout; the wall

[a] *Prob. rdg.; Heb. adds* the fighting men.

of the city will collapse and the army shall advance, every
man straight ahead.' So Joshua son of Nun summoned 6
the priests and gave them their orders: 'Take up the Ark
of the Covenant; let seven priests with seven trumpets
of ram's horn go in front of the Ark of the LORD.' Then 7
he said to the army, 'March on and make the circuit of
the city, and let the men drafted from the two and a half
tribes go in front of the Ark of the LORD.' When Joshua 8
had spoken to the army, the seven priests carrying the
seven trumpets of ram's horn before the LORD passed on
and blew the trumpets, with the Ark of the Covenant
of the LORD following them. The drafted men marched 9
in front of the priests who blew the trumpets, and the
rearguard followed the Ark, the trumpets sounding as
they marched. But Joshua ordered the army not to shout, 10
or to raise their voices or utter a word, till the day came
when he would tell them to shout; then they were to
give a loud shout. Thus he caused the Ark of the LORD to 11
go round the city, making the circuit of it once, and then
they went back to the camp and spent the night there.
Joshua rose early in the morning and the priests took up 12
the Ark of the LORD. The seven priests carrying the seven 13
trumpets of ram's horn went marching in front of the
Ark of the LORD, blowing the trumpets as they went,
with the drafted men in front of them and the rearguard
following the Ark of the LORD, the trumpets sounding
as they marched. They marched round the city once on 14
the second day and returned to the camp; this they did
for six days. But on the seventh day they rose at dawn 15
and marched seven times round the city in the same way;
that was the only day on which they marched round

16 seven times. The seventh time the priests blew the trumpets and Joshua said to the army, 'Shout! The LORD has
17 given you the city. The city shall be under solemn ban: everything in it belongs to the LORD. No one is to be spared except the prostitute Rahab and everyone who is with her in the house, because she hid the men whom we
18 sent. And you must beware of coveting[a] anything that is forbidden under the ban; you must take none of it for yourselves; this would put the Israelite camp itself under
19 the ban and bring trouble on it. All the silver and gold, all the vessels of copper and iron, shall be holy; they belong to the LORD and they must go into the LORD's
20 treasury.' So[b] they blew the trumpets, and when the army heard the trumpet sound, they raised a great shout, and down fell the walls. The army advanced on the city,
21 every man straight ahead, and took it. Under the ban they destroyed everything in the city; they put everyone to the sword, men and women, young and old, and also cattle, sheep, and asses.

22 But the two men who had been sent out as spies were told by Joshua to go into the prostitute's house and bring out her and all who belonged to her, as they had sworn
23 to do. So the young men went and brought out Rahab, her father and mother, her brothers and all who belonged to her. They brought out the whole family and left them
24 outside the Israelite camp. They then set fire to the city and everything in it, except that they deposited the silver and gold and the vessels of copper and iron in the treasury
25 of the LORD's house. Thus Joshua spared the lives of

[a] *So Sept.; Heb.* putting under the ban.
[b] *So Sept.; Heb. adds* the people shouted and...

Rahab the prostitute, her household and all who belonged
to her, because she had hidden the men whom Joshua had
sent to Jericho as spies; she and her family settled permanently among the Israelites. It was then that Joshua 26
laid this curse on Jericho:

> May the LORD's curse light on the man who comes
>   forward
>   to rebuild this city of Jericho:
> the laying of its foundations shall cost him his eldest son,
> the setting up of its gates shall cost him his youngest.

Thus the LORD was with Joshua, and his fame spread 27
throughout the country.

✻ This chapter resumes the story of ch. 2, reporting the
destruction of Jericho and the preservation of Rahab and her
family. The narrative follows a familiar pattern. After noting
that Jericho was under siege (verse 1), it reports the LORD's
instructions to Joshua (verses 2–5), Joshua's communication
of those orders to the priests and the army (verses 6–7), the
careful execution of the plan with the expected collapse of
the city walls (verses 8–21), and the results of the attack,
including the rescue of Rahab and her household (verses 22–7).

While the sequence of events is clearer than in chs. 2–4,
there are difficulties in the narrative which suggest that it has
passed through many different hands before reaching its
present form. First, the order of events is slightly problematic.
There is no report of the Israelite advance upon the city, and
Joshua interrupts the action to give further instructions in
verses 10 and 17–19. Second, there are several duplicates: two
reports of the final blast of the trumpets (verses 16 and 20),
two accounts of the destruction of the city (verses 21 and 24),
two signals for the shout (the trumpet blast, verses 5 and 20,
and Joshua's command, verses 10 and 16), and two accounts
of the rescue of Rahab (verses 22–3 and 25). Third, did the

walls fall at the sound of the trumpet or the shout of the army? Fourth, verses 9*b* and 13*b* in the Hebrew text leave open the possibility that it was the rearguard behind the Ark which was sounding the trumpets and not the priests. Fifth, while parts of the story depend directly upon the agreement with Rahab, the basic account of the destruction of the walls does not remember that the prostitute's house was built against the wall (cp. 2: 15 and the note on 2: 15–21).

The diverse oral and written traditions which comprise the story are not easy to disentangle. Only a few verses (e.g. 27) can be assigned to the Deuteronomistic editor. Very probably one old tradition described a silent march around the city with the walls falling at the shout of the people. Another tradition or traditions spoke of the Ark, the priests and the trumpets. The story of Rahab was probably yet another account of the capture of Jericho.

In view of the literary difficulties, it is not reasonable to expect the story to preserve accurate historical details. Archaeologists have searched without success for evidence of the walls that fell down. The most recent and most scientific excavation of the city in 1952–8 found no evidence that the city was occupied during the most likely period of the conquest. Two previous excavators thought they had discovered evidence of a city destroyed by Joshua but their dates were mistaken by several hundred years.

This story was not written as history. Its primary purpose is to make an affirmation of faith in the God who can lead his people to victory in war. Because of divine activity and human obedience, the first success in Canaan was the most dramatic and most complete. The basic theme of divine activity is strengthened by the presence of numerous liturgical elements. These include the Ark, the priests, the trumpet-blasts, the procession around the city, the repeated use of the sacred number seven, the placing of the city under 'solemn ban', and the general mood of a high religious occasion.

Some scholars have concluded that the story had been

strongly influenced by the liturgy of a particular ceremony, but concrete evidence for such a celebration is lacking. It seems much more likely that the account has been shaped to a great extent by the institution and ideas of the holy war. (For laws concerning such warfare, see Deut. 20.) In the holy war, no battle could begin without religious ceremonies in which the will of God was determined and the army consecrated. The soldiers were not professionals but ordinary Israelite men summoned to fight by the sound of the trumpet; their leader had to be called by the LORD. The presence of the LORD at the head of the army was often symbolized by the Ark. While the enemies trembled before the army (cp. 2: 9; 5: 1), the Israelites were encouraged to stand firm and have no fear. The victory was usually accomplished by a miracle accompanied by a war-cry; the enemy was thrown into panic. All the spoils of the battle belonged to the LORD; except in special circumstances (for example, the agreement with Rahab) all living things were to be killed and all property destroyed except what was taken to the LORD's treasury. While it is not always possible to separate historical fact from theological ideas in the holy-war traditions, it is known that such stories reflect a military institution (with non-professional soldiers and divinely ordained leaders) which was practised in the period before the monarchy. Some features of the institution were revived for a time by Josiah (640–609 B.C.).

The chapter concludes with two aetiologies. On the one hand, it explains the presence of the descendants of Rahab within Israel (verses 22–5, see comments on ch. 2); on the other, it explains why Jericho was never rebuilt (verse 26).

1. On the location of *Jericho* see the note on 2: 1. The city was under siege; for laws concerning the conduct of a siege, see Deut. 20: 19–20.

2. *Look, I have delivered*: the formula signified that the victory has already been accomplished by divine will (cp. verse 16). The expression is common in the holy war stories.

3. The Septuagint text is shorter, suggesting that the Israelites did not march around the city but surrounded it.

4. The number *seven* which recurs so many times in this story was sacred in ancient Israel as in the ancient Near East in general. The source of its sacredness is unknown. The importance of the number in religious ceremonies is related to the weekly cycle, specifically the Sabbath (cp. Gen. 2: 1–3). The *seventh day* in this context probably was the Sabbath.

On the *Ark*, see the note on Josh. 3: 3.

trumpets made from rams' horns: such instruments were commonly used in warfare (see 2 Chron. 13: 13ff.) and in services of worship (see Num. 10: 1–10; Ps. 47: 5). They also sounded to herald the beginning of the fiftieth or jubilee year (see Lev. 25: 9).

5. *the whole army*: literally, 'all the people'; similarly in verses 7, 8, 10, 16, and 20.

7. *men drafted from the two and a half tribes*: literally, 'drafted men', or 'chosen men' (cp. verses 9 and 13). The N.E.B. has interpreted this word as a reference to the warriors of the Transjordanian tribes (see 1: 12–15).

8. Here the LORD himself goes with the people; elsewhere his presence is symbolized by the Ark.

11. The location of *the camp* is not specified; the context suggests that it was in nearby Gilgal (see 5: 10 and the note on 4: 19).

17–19. The meaning of the *solemn ban* (*ḥērem*) is explained. Since the enemy and the booty belong to the LORD, they are sacred or taboo. To take possession of such things would be similar to approaching too close to God himself. The *solemn ban* is not limited to the holy war; private property could be 'devoted' to the LORD (see Lev. 27: 26–9), and an Israelite who sacrificed to a foreign god was to be put to death under 'solemn ban' (Exod. 22: 20). Holiness is contagious; if one person takes what is forbidden he will endanger the *Israelite camp* itself (ch. 7 and Num. 31: 7–20). Deut. 21: 10-14 allows some captives taken in war to be spared, but does not appear to include cases such as the present one. In speaking of the rescue of Rahab and her family, the present story attempts to reconcile the fact that Canaanites continued to live within Israel with the theological idea that they were all to be killed.

The brutal practice of slaughtering all the enemy was not limited to Israel. In the Moabite stone, King Mesha (ninth century B.C.) testifies that he destroyed the city of Ataroth and slew all its inhabitants as a sacrifice to his god Chemosh.

18. *bring trouble*: the language anticipates the conclusion of the story of Achan (see especially 7: 24–6).

24. *LORD's house*: an apparent reference to the temple in Jerusalem, perhaps a late scribal addition to the text. The first temple was not in fact built until the time of Solomon (about 961 B.C.), some 300 years after the conquest.

25. *settled permanently among the Israelites*: literally, 'and she lives in Israel to this day'. The formula 'to this day' is common in aetiologies (see the comment on 4: 9).

26. The *curse* explains why Jericho never was rebuilt. The precise fulfilment of the curse is reported in 1 Kings 16: 34 when Hiel of Bethel tried to rebuild the city. One of these texts depends directly upon the other, but it is not possible to determine which. The Deuteronomistic historian frequently shows how threats such as this one were fulfilled, or how disasters had been prophesied in advance.

ACHAN'S SIN

But the Israelites defied the ban: Achan son of Carmi, **7** son of Zabdi, son of Zerah, of the tribe of Judah, took some of the forbidden things, and the LORD was angry with the Israelites.

Joshua sent men from Jericho with orders to go up to 2 Ai, near Beth-aven, east of Bethel, and see how the land lay; so the men went up and explored Ai. They returned 3

to Joshua and reported that there was no need for the whole army to move: 'Let some two or three thousand men go forward to attack Ai. Do not make the whole
4 army toil up there; the population is small.' And so about three thousand men went up, but they turned tail before
5 the men of Ai, who killed some thirty-six of them; they chased them all the way from the gate to the Quarries*a* and killed them on the pass. At this the courage of the
6 people melted and flowed away like water. Joshua and the elders of Israel rent their clothes and flung themselves face downwards to the ground; they lay before the Ark of the LORD till evening and threw dust on their heads.
7 Joshua said, 'Alas, O Lord GOD, why didst thou bring this people across the Jordan only to hand us over to the Amorites to be destroyed? If only we had been content
8 to settle on the other side of the Jordan! I beseech thee, O Lord; what can I say, now that Israel has been routed
9 by the enemy? When the Canaanites and all the natives of the country hear of this, they will come swarming around us and wipe us off the face of the earth. What wilt thou do then for the honour of thy great name?'
10 The LORD said to Joshua, 'Stand up; why lie prostrate
11 on your face? Israel has sinned: they have broken the covenant which I laid upon them, by taking forbidden things for themselves. They have stolen them, and concealed it by mingling them with their own possessions.
12 That is why the Israelites cannot stand against their enemies: they are put to flight because they have brought themselves under the ban. Unless they destroy every single thing among them that is forbidden under the ban,

[*a*] *Or* to Shebarim.

I will be with them no longer. Stand up; you must 13
hallow the people; tell them they must hallow themselves
for tomorrow. Tell them, These are the words of the
LORD the God of Israel: You have forbidden things
among you, Israel; you cannot stand against your enemies
until you have rid yourselves of them. In the morning 14
come forward tribe by tribe, and the tribe which the
LORD chooses shall come forward clan by clan; the clan
which the LORD chooses shall come forward family by
family; and the family which the LORD chooses shall
come forward man by man. The man who is chosen as 15
the harbourer of forbidden things shall be burnt, he and
all that is his, because he has broken the covenant of the
LORD and committed outrage in Israel.' Early in the 16
morning Joshua rose and brought Israel forward tribe by
tribe, and the tribe of Judah was chosen. He brought 17
forward the clans of Judah, and the clan of Zerah was
chosen; then the clan of Zerah family by family,*a* and
the family of*b* Zabdi was chosen. He brought that family 18
forward man by man, and Achan son of Carmi, son of
Zabdi, son of Zerah, of the tribe of Judah, was chosen.
Then Joshua said to Achan, 'My son, give honour to the 19
LORD the God of Israel and make your confession to him:
tell me what you have done, hide nothing from me.'
Achan answered Joshua, 'I confess, I have sinned against 20
the LORD the God of Israel. This is what I did: among the 21
booty I caught sight of a fine mantle from Shinar, two
hundred shekels of silver, and a bar of gold weighing
fifty shekels. I coveted them and I took them. You will

[*a*] *So some MSS.; others* man by man.
[*b*] the family of: *so Sept.; Heb. om.*

find them hidden in the ground inside my tent, with the
22 silver underneath.' So Joshua sent messengers, who ran
to the tent, and there was the stuff[a] hidden in the tent
23 with the silver underneath. They took the things from
the tent, brought them to Joshua and all the Israelites, and
24 spread them out before the LORD. Then Joshua took
Achan son of Zerah, with the silver, the mantle, and the
bar of gold, together with his sons and daughters, his
oxen, his asses, and his sheep, his tent, and everything he
had, and he and all Israel brought them up to the Vale
25 of Achor.[b] Joshua said, 'What trouble you have brought
on us! Now the LORD will bring trouble on you.' Then
26 all the Israelites stoned him to death;[c] and they raised a
great pile of stones over him, which remains to this day.
So the LORD's anger was abated. That is why to this day
that place is called the Vale of Achor.

✴ Chs. 7 and 8 could be read together as the account of two
campaigns against the city of Ai, the first a failure and the
second a success. But the chapters actually preserve two distinct stories, which, nevertheless, had been combined long
before the time of the Deuteronomistic historian. While it
also reports the first attack on Ai, the main theme of ch. 7
is the trial and execution of Achan. 8: 1–29, on the other hand,
focuses entirely upon the defeat of Ai. Two localities are
involved in chs. 7 and 8. The setting of the Achan story is the
vicinity of Jericho and Gilgal; most of the Israelites – perhaps
even Joshua himself – remained there while a small force
carried out an attack on Ai. In ch. 8 the scene moves from the
Jordan valley to the hill-country. Furthermore, the Achan
story is related as closely to ch. 6 as it is to ch. 8. The grounds

[a] *Or* the mantle.   [b] *That is* Trouble.
[c] *So Sept.; Heb. adds* and they burnt them with fire and pelted them
with stones.

for the defeat and the trial were laid in the instructions concerning the 'solemn ban', specifically in 6: 18: 'you must take none of it for yourselves; this would put the Israelite camp itself under the ban and bring trouble on it'.

The story tells how one man violated one commandment and the entire people suffered. Achan took some of the things forbidden by the ban (verse 1), and consequently Israel lost the next battle (verses 2–5). After Joshua mourns the defeat and prays (verses 6–9), the LORD reveals that someone has sinned and gives instructions for discovering the offender (verses 10–15). Joshua carries out the instructions, discovers Achan and has him executed, restoring the proper relationship with the LORD (verses 16–26). The account includes two aetiologies: it explains the name 'Vale of Achor' (verses 24, 26) and a remarkable 'pile of stones' (verse 26).

These aetiologies may have given rise to the tradition, or they may be late additions to the story. Nevertheless, in the present context the basic purpose of the story is not to answer questions concerning the origin of a name or a tomb. The main point of the narrative as a whole is that obedience to God's commands leads to success, and disobedience – even by a single individual – results in failure. Achan – and the valley of Achor – is a lesson to all future Israelites, not only those who participate in the holy war, but also all who are faced with the question of obedience or disobedience to the law. This chapter illustrates failure; chs. 6 and 8 show the opposite side of the coin. While there is little or no Deuteronomistic editing here, the story suits the ideas of the editor perfectly. Retribution is a common theme in this history (see above, p. 15) and in Deuteronomy: 'Know then that the LORD your God is God, the faithful God; with those who love him and keep his commandments he keeps covenant and faith for a thousand generations, but those who defy him and show their hatred for him he repays with destruction: he will not be slow to requite any who so hate him' (Deut. 7: 9–10). Furthermore, this idea of reward and punishment is ancient and common in Israel. (Nevertheless it did not go un-challenged, as the books of Job and Ecclesiastes testify.)

1. *the Israelites defied the ban*: one man sinned but all were guilty and the entire nation suffered. See also verses 10 and 11: 'Israel has sinned; they have broken the covenant.' Under-lying these words and the chapter as a whole is the idea of corporate guilt. The entire community could be – and often was – punished for the crime of a single individual. In 2 Sam. 21: 1–10 a famine in the time of David is explained as the result of a crime committed by Saul and his family. In the present story, the idea that the group suffers because of an individual's sin is intensified because the 'solemn ban' is involved. Since holy things can affect all who come too near them, the entire camp is contaminated. The punishment of Achan therefore becomes a ritual of purification; by removing the guilty party (and his family), Joshua removes the guilt (cp. verse 26).

2. *Ai, near Beth-aven, east of Bethel*: the text originally spoke of only two places; *Beth-aven* is a gloss on the text. It does not occur in the Septuagint, and elsewhere there seems to be some confusion between the names Bethel and Beth-aven (cp. 16: 1–2; 18: 12–13). Beth-aven, which means 'house of taboo', seems to be an insulting substitute for Bethel, 'house of God', which was considered the site of false worship (cp. Hos. 4: 15; 10: 5). *Ai* (identified with et-Tell) is 2–3 kilo-metres (about 1½ miles) east of Bethel (identified with Beitin). See Map 1 and the Gazetteer. A very important sanctuary was located at Bethel; the establishment of the holy place was traced to Jacob's dream of a ladder which reached to heaven (Gen. 28: 10–22). The relationship between Bethel and 'Luz', with which it is identified on two occasions, is uncertain (see the note on 18: 12–13).

see how the land lay: literally, 'spy out the land'. See the note on 2: 1.

5. Since *thirty-six* Israelites died, Achan was indirectly guilty of murder. However, this point is not mentioned in his

accusation; since his crime was against the LORD, it was considered more serious than murder.

the pass: or 'the descent'. The Israelites fled from the Judaean hills down one of the many ravines to the Jordan valley.

6. *Joshua and the elders* begin the ritual of mourning for Israel's loss. In addition to tearing the clothes, falling to the ground (cp. Job 1 : 20), and putting dust on the head, mourning could include dressing in sackcloth, beating the breast, engaging in a fast (Joel 1 : 8–14) or even shaving the head and cutting the body (Jer. 16: 6–7). Many of the same rituals are appropriate in connection with prayers of petition, such as the one which follows in verses 7–9. When David's son by Bathsheba became ill, he prayed, fasted, and lay on the ground (2 Sam. 12: 15–16).

7–9. Joshua offers a prayer of complaint and petition. He bemoans the loss, implying that God is to blame (verse 7), and gives reasons why God should help Israel: if his people are destroyed, there will be none to praise his *great name*. These motifs are common in complaint-psalms. The language recalls Israel's complaints against Moses and the LORD in the wilderness (cp. Exod. 16: 2–8).

11. *the covenant* (i.e. sworn agreement) implied here would have included the LORD's commitment to defeat the enemies and Israel's promise to dedicate all the spoils to their God.

13. *hallow the people*: see the note to 3: 5.

14. The legal procedure is a trial by sacred lot. In Israel as well as the ancient Near East in general many cases were resolved by being brought 'before God' (cp. Exod. 22: 9). The phrase, *which the LORD chooses*, refers to the casting of the lot, though the particular procedure is not described. In Israel, casting lots was used to discern God's will concerning various questions. The tribal boundaries were assigned by lot (14: 2; 18: 6), Saul was chosen king by lot (1 Sam. 10: 19–24), and Jonah's guilt was discovered by lot (Jonah 1: 7).

15. God commands that the guilty man and his household

be burnt; the N.E.B. (following the Septuagint) of verse 25 reports only that he was stoned, but the Hebrew text of verse 25 says he was both stoned and burnt. Elsewhere in the Old Testament burning is mentioned as punishment for certain crimes (cp. Gen. 38: 24; Lev. 21: 9).

20. Achan's confession and the evidence which it brings to light (verse 22) confirm the decision reached by lot.

21. *Shinar*: lower Mesopotamia, the region of the city of Babylon. In Israelite times the shekel weighed about 11½ grams (4 ounces).

25. See the note on verse 15.

The prophet Hosea and his listeners obviously knew this story:

> there I will restore her vineyards,
> turning the Vale of Trouble into the Gate of Hope
> (Hos. 2: 15*a*).

26. Achan was given the burial of a criminal as was the king of Ai (8: 29), and Absalom (2 Sam. 18: 17).

The aetiology of *Vale of Achor* is a play on the words 'Achor' and 'Achan'. According to 15: 7, the Vale of Achor was located on the boundary between Judah and Benjamin. This location corresponds to the identification of Achan as a Judaean in verse 1. ✳

THE CONQUEST OF AI

8 The LORD said to Joshua, 'Do not be fearful or dismayed; take the whole army and attack Ai. I deliver the king of Ai into your hands, him and his people, his city
2 and his country. Deal with Ai and her king as you dealt with Jericho and her king; but you may keep for yourselves the cattle and any other spoil that you may take.
3 Set an ambush for the city to the west of it.' So Joshua and all the army prepared for the assault on Ai. He chose

thirty thousand fighting men and dispatched them by
night, with these orders: 'Lie in ambush to the west of 4
the city, not far from it, and all of you hold yourselves
in readiness. I myself will approach the city with the 5
rest of the army, and when the enemy come out to meet
us as they did last time, we shall take to flight before them.
Then they will come out and pursue us until we have 6
drawn them away from the city, thinking that we have
taken to flight as we did last time. While we are in flight,
come out from your ambush and occupy the city; the 7
LORD your God will deliver it into your hands. When 8
you have taken it, set it on fire. Thus you will do what the
LORD commands. These are your orders.' So Joshua sent 9
them off, and they went to the place of ambush and
waited between Bethel and Ai to the west of Ai, while
Joshua spent the night with the army.

Early in the morning Joshua rose, mustered the army 10
and marched against Ai, he himself and the elders of
Israel at its head. All the armed forces with him marched 11
on until they came within sight of the city. They encamped north of Ai, with the valley between them and
the city; but Joshua took some five thousand men and 12
set them in ambush between Bethel and Ai to the west of
the city.[a] When the king of Ai saw them, he and the 14
citizens rose with all speed that morning and marched out
to do battle against Israel;[b] he did not know that there
was an ambush set for him to the west of the city. Joshua 15
and all the Israelites made as if they were routed by them

[a] *So Sept.; Heb. adds* (13) So the army pitched camp to the north of
the city, and the rearguard to the west, while Joshua went that night
into the valley.
[b] *So Sept.; Heb. adds* for the appointed time, before the Arabah.

16 and fled towards the wilderness, and all the people in the
city were called out in pursuit. So they pursued Joshua
17 and were drawn away from the city. Not a man was left
in Ai;[a] they had all gone out in pursuit of the Israelites
and during the pursuit had left the city undefended.
18 Then the LORD said to Joshua, 'Point towards Ai with
the dagger you are holding, for I will deliver the city
into your hands.' So Joshua pointed with his dagger
19 towards Ai. At his signal, the men in ambush rose quickly
from their places and, entering the city at a run, took it
20 and promptly set fire to it. The men of Ai looked back
and saw the smoke from the city already going up to the
sky; they were powerless to make their escape in any
direction, and the Israelites who had feigned flight towards
21 the wilderness turned on their pursuers. For when Joshua
and all the Israelites saw that the ambush had seized the
city and that smoke was already going up from it, they
22 turned and fell upon the men of Ai. Those who had
come out to meet the Israelites were now hemmed in
with Israelites on both sides of them, and the Israelites
cut them down until there was not a single survivor, nor
23 had any escaped. The king of Ai was taken alive and
24 brought to Joshua. When the Israelites had cut down to
the last man all the citizens of Ai who were in the open
country or in the wilderness to which they had pursued
them, and the massacre was complete, they all turned
25 back to Ai and put it to the sword. The number who
were killed that day, men and women, was twelve
26 thousand, the whole population of Ai. Joshua held out
his dagger and did not draw back his hand until he had

[a] So Sept.; Heb. adds or Bethel.

put to death all who lived in Ai; but the Israelites kept 27
for themselves the cattle and any other spoil that they
took, following the word of the LORD spoken to Joshua.
So Joshua burnt Ai to the ground, and left it the desolate 28
ruined mound it remains to this day. He hanged the king 29
of Ai on a tree and left him there till sunset; and when the
sun had set, he gave the order and they cut him down and
flung down his body at the entrance of the city gate.
Over the body they raised a great pile of stones, which
is there to this day.

* After the interruption for the trial and execution of Achan,
the story of the war of conquest continues. The second city
reported captured and destroyed by Joshua and the Israelites
was Ai. In the context, the story of this victory is presented as
the second attack on the city, the sequel to ch. 7. However,
this narrative can easily be read and understood without
reference to the previous chapter, and it doubtless circulated
alone before it was combined with the other conquest stories.
There are, however, connecting motifs in the allusions to the
'flight' of the Israelites and the pursuit by the people of Ai
in both chapters (8: 6–7, 15–16, and 7: 4–5). It seems likely
that the story of the failure depends upon the tradition of the
success.

The account includes the following elements: verses 1–9
report the LORD's instructions and Joshua's preparations, including the plans for an ambush. Verses 10–17 report the
setting of the ambush and the success of the tactics. The final
paragraph (verses 18–29) gives an account of the actual attack
upon Ai and the destruction of the city, and two aetiologies
(verses 28–9) conclude the report: they explain the name of
the city and a 'great pile of stones' at its entrance.

Though the chapter reports a complex sequence of events,
it is possible to follow most of the steps along the way.
Nevertheless, as in most of the previous stories, there are

sufficient difficulties to suggest that the story is the result of the combination of two or more traditions, and that other additions have been made as it was handed down. In this case most of the difficulties are duplicates: there are two reports of the beginning (verses 3 and 10), two accounts of setting the ambush (verses 9 and 12), two different numbers given for the troops (verses 3 and 12), two references to the encampment at Ai (verses 12 and 13), and two reports of the burning of the city (verses 19 and 28). The two aetiologies have already been mentioned. In addition to the two or more traditions revealed by these repetitions, the hand of the Deuteronomistic editor may be visible in verses 1 (cp. Deut. 3: 2) and 2 (cp. Deut. 3: 7).

The tradition clearly interprets the victory as the work of the LORD – according to verses 1–2, the strategy had been given as a divine revelation – and the battle as another phase of the holy war: the victory is total, the enemy is thrown into panic (verses 20ff.), and all the citizens of Ai are killed (see comments on ch. 6). Nevertheless, in significant ways the story differs from the account of the capture of Jericho, and from holy-war stories in general. The victory is accomplished by shrewd tactics instead of a miracle, there is no reference to the presence of the Ark or the LORD at the head of the army, liturgical features (e.g. a procession, priests, trumpets) are missing, and an exception is made in the rule of the 'solemn ban': the Israelites are allowed to keep the 'spoil' for themselves (verse 27). This last point is especially striking in view of the crime of Achan reported in the previous chapter.

Archaeological excavations at Ai have cast serious doubt upon the historical reliability of this narrative. Excavations in 1933–4 proved that there was a great walled city there during the Late Bronze Age, but it had been destroyed perhaps as much as a millennium before the Israelites arrived on the scene. These results have been confirmed by a recent American expedition. There was only sparse settlement in the Iron Age, long after the period of the conquest. Therefore, the city was a ruin when the Israelites arrived, and so remained during most of the history of Israel. Some scholars have attempted to resolve the difficulty posed by this evidence by suggesting that ch. 8 originally reported the destruction of Bethel, not Ai. This suggestion, however, seems most unlikely. The geographical references in the story are too detailed and too accurate to support such a theory. In view of the archaeological evidence, the aetiological conclusions and the name of the city itself (see comment on verse 1), it seems most likely that the need to explain the name of the place contributed significantly to the development and preservation of this account.

1. *Ai*: the Hebrew (*hāʿai*) means, literally, 'the ruin'. The word actually is not a proper name but a common noun. There can be very little question concerning the identification of this place with the et-Tell, 'the ruin'. (On the location of the city and its relationship to Bethel see the note on 7: 2.) In view of this detailed story of the destruction of the city, it is somewhat surprising that Ai is not mentioned in the boundary descriptions, though the line passes in its immediate vicinity (cp. 16: 2; 18: 12–13). The silence of the boundary list is consistent with the archaeological evidence (see above) that the city was occupied only briefly and sparsely after the Israelites arrived in Palestine. Like Gilgal and Jericho, Ai was located within the territory of the tribe of Benjamin. The fact that thus far in the book of Joshua all the events have taken place within Benjamite territory supports the conclusion that most of the conquest stories came from that tribe's special traditions which were preserved at Gilgal (see above, p. 8).

Do not be fearful or dismayed: a common formula in the holy-war tradition (cp. 6: 2; Exod. 14: 13).

2. *Jericho and her king*: the account of the destruction of Jericho did not refer specifically to a king, though one appears in the story of Rahab and the spies (2: 2ff.).

The ambush *west* of the city would have placed it between Ai and Bethel (see the note on 7: 2).

3. *all the army*: see comments on 6: 5.

11–13. There is some confusion concerning the location of the two parts of the army, probably as a result of the combination of traditions.

13. The N.E.B. follows the Septuagint in omitting this verse, which probably was an explanatory scribal addition.

17. Again, the N.E.B. follows the Septuagint; the Hebrew reads, 'Not a man was left in Ai or Bethel.'

18–19. Joshua's *signal* recalls the action of Moses during the war with Amalek (Exod. 17: 8–13). As long as Moses kept his staff raised the Israelites 'had the advantage' in the battle. This is one more incident in the life of Joshua which parallels the career of Moses.

28–9. On the formula, *to this day*, see comments on 4: 9.

29. *the king of Ai* was treated as a criminal. He was executed, left on public display and his body cast in the *city gate* where it was buried under *a great pile of stones*. The five kings who opposed Joshua were treated similarly (10: 26–7). The removal of the body at *sunset* is in accordance with the law in Deut. 21: 22–3 which orders that a condemned man should be buried on the same day he is executed. ✶

A CEREMONY ON MOUNT EBAL

30 At that time Joshua built an altar to the LORD the God
31 of Israel on Mount Ebal. The altar was of blocks of undressed stone on which no tool of iron had been used, following the commands given to the Israelites by Moses the servant of the LORD, as is described in the book of the law of Moses. At the altar they offered whole-offerings
32 to the LORD, and slaughtered shared-offerings. There in the presence of the Israelites he engraved on blocks[a] of
33 stone a copy of the law of Moses.[b] And all Israel, elders,

[a] Or on the blocks.　　[b] So Sept.; Heb. adds which he had engraved.

officers, and judges, took their stand on either side of the Ark, facing the levitical priests who carried the Ark of the Covenant of the LORD – all Israel, native and alien alike. Half of them stood facing Mount Gerizim and half facing Mount Ebal, to fulfil the command of Moses the servant of the LORD that the blessing should be pronounced first. Then Joshua recited the whole of the 34 blessing and the cursing word by word, as they are written in the book of the law. There was not a single 35 word of all that Moses had commanded which he did not read aloud before the whole congregation of Israel, including the women and dependants and the aliens resident in their company.

✻ It is difficult to explain the presence of the report of the establishment of an altar 'on Mount Ebal' at this particular point in the story of the conquest. From Ai the Israelites would have to move 32 kilometres (about 20 miles) almost directly north for their peaceful ceremony and the establishment of a sanctuary. But though the defeat of Ai could have opened the route to the north, there has been no report of the capture of the region of 'Mount Ebal'. Indeed, there is no account of the capture of this hill-country in the territory of the Joseph tribes except the brief and confusing note in 17: 14–18 (see comments there). Furthermore, the context reads more smoothly with the omission of this account. At 9: 6 it is assumed that Joshua and the people are back in their camp in Gilgal, and tells of a treaty with the people of Gibeon, which is just a few miles south of Ai. The Septuagint has the paragraph after 9: 3, but this does not relieve the tension. Some modern commentators, recognizing that the unit treats of the same events at the same place as ch. 24, put it with the latter chapter, perhaps after 24: 27. But the Deuteronomistic editor has told the story at this point, early in the account of the conquest, probably because of the importance which he attached to the ceremony and to the location. As soon as the road to the north was opened, the ceremony at this place should be performed.

The paragraph reports the building of an altar on Mount Ebal, the presentation of offerings, the inscription of 'a copy of the law of Moses' on stone, and the recital of 'the blessing and the cursing' – and perhaps the law as well. Most of these acts are part of the covenant renewal ceremony (for details see comments on 24: 1–28).   *

Most recent commentators correctly conclude that the passage, though it contains evidence of an old tradition, stems primarily from the Deuteronomistic historian. The paragraph reports the fulfilment of the instructions given in Deut. 27, and contains several exact verbal parallels to that chapter and Deut. 11: 29. Evidence for an older tradition is the confusion concerning the exact location of the ceremony (see note on verse 30). That tradition included at least the instructions for building an altar.

30. *Mount Ebal*: the text is unclear about the place of the events: the altar was on the mount, but according to verse 33, half the people faced the mountain. The people would have been standing in Shechem, definitely identified with Tell Balatah near Nablus (see Map 1 and the Gazetteer). The city stood in the pass between Mount Ebal and Mount Gerizim (verse 33). Shechem was one of the most ancient and important centres of worship in early Israel; according to ch. 24 it was the site of a covenant ceremony.

31. *the book of the law of Moses*: it is not known which 'book' the writer has in mind; the instructions here follow the law recorded in Exod. 20: 25.

32. *engraved on blocks*: were these the same stones which formed the altar? The Hebrew (literally, 'on the stones') suggests that the same stones were used, but to engrave them would violate the instructions in verse 31 and Exod. 20: 25. Moses' instructions for setting up 'great stones' and inscribing

'on them all the words of this law' are found in Deut. 27: 2–3. Writing the law frequently is associated with the covenant ceremony (cp. Exod. 24: 3–8; 34; Josh. 24: 25ff.).

33. According to *the command of Moses* in Deut. 27: 13, some of the tribes were to stand on Mount Ebal and some on Mount Gerizim. *

ISRAEL'S ENEMIES UNITE

When the news of these happenings reached all the **9** kings west of the Jordan, in the hill-country, the Shephelah, and all the coast of the Great Sea running up to the Lebanon, the kings of the Hittites, Amorites, Canaanites, Perizzites, Hivites, and Jebusites agreed to join forces **2** and fight against Joshua and Israel.

* With this brief summary of Israel's enemies west of the Jordan the Deuteronomistic editor introduces chs. 9–11. His statement envisages an alliance of all the rulers of the diverse and independent city states of Palestine. But the summary is not entirely consistent with the material which follows. The remainder of ch. 9 reports how one city sought and won peace with Israel, ch. 10 tells of the defeat of a coalition of five cities in the southern hill-country, and ch. 11 gives an account of the destruction of Hazor and her allies in the north. This statement, in short, is more grandiose than the sum of the individual stories. The editor has a tendency to exaggerate and simplify events, and does so in similar transitional passages throughout the book (cp. 10: 40–2; 11: 16–20).

1. *the hill-country, the Shephelah, and all the coast of the Great Sea running up to the Lebanon*: this phrase is presented as a characterization of the entire land *west of the Jordan*, and in general it includes the major topographical divisions. More specifically, however, it best describes the central region. There is some variation in details among the editor's de-

scriptions of the land. In 11: 16–17 (see comment) is a more lengthy list of regions, but it omits *the coast of the Great Sea*. In fact, Israel was unable to control the coastal region until David subdued the Philistine cities.

the Hittites, Amorites, Canaanites, Perizzites, Hivites, and Jebusites: see the comment on 3: 10. This list differs from the one in 3: 10 in the order of the names and the omission of 'the Girgashites'. ✳

THE TREATY WITH THE GIBEONITES

3 When the inhabitants of Gibeon heard how Joshua had
4 dealt with Jericho and Ai, they adopted a ruse of their own. They went and disguised themselves, with old sacking
5 for their asses, old wine-skins split and mended, old and patched sandals for their feet, old clothing to wear, and by way of provisions nothing but dry and mouldy bread.
6 They came to Joshua in the camp at Gilgal and said to him and the Israelites, 'We have come from a distant
7 country to ask you now to grant us a treaty.' The Israelites said to the Hivites, 'But maybe you live in our neighbourhood: if so, how can we grant you a treaty?'
8 They said to Joshua, 'We are your slaves.' Joshua asked
9 them who they were and where they came from. 'Sir,' they replied, 'our country is very far away, and we have come because of the renown of the LORD your God. We
10 have heard of his fame, of all that he did to Egypt, and to the two Amorite kings east of the Jordan, Sihon king of Heshbon and Og king of Bashan who lived at Ash-
11 taroth. Our elders and all the people of our country told us to take provisions for the journey and come to meet you, and say, "We are your slaves; please grant us a

treaty." Look at our bread; it was hot from the oven 12
when we packed it at home on the day we came away.
Now it is dry and mouldy. Look at the wine-skins; they 13
were new when we filled them, and now they are all
split; look at our clothes and our sandals, worn out by
the long journey.' The chief men[a] of the community 14
accepted some of their provisions, and did not at first
seek guidance from the LORD. So Joshua received them 15
peaceably and granted them a treaty, promising to spare
their lives, and the chiefs pledged their faith to them on
oath.

Within three days of granting them the treaty, the 16
Israelites learnt that they were in fact neighbours and
lived near by. So the Israelites set out and on the third 17
day they reached their cities; these were Gibeon, Kephirah, Beeroth, and Kiriath-jearim. The Israelites did not 18
slaughter them, because of the oath which the chief men
of the community had sworn to them by the LORD the
God of Israel, but the people were all indignant with their
chiefs. The chiefs all replied to the assembled people, 19
'But we swore an oath to them by the LORD the God of
Israel; we cannot touch them now. What we will do is 20
this: we will spare their lives so that the oath which we
swore to them may bring no harm upon us.[b] But though 21
their lives must be spared, they shall be[c] set to chop wood
and draw water for the community.' The people agreed
to do[d] as their chiefs had said. Joshua summoned the 22
Gibeonites and said, 'Why did you play this trick on us?

[a] *So Sept.; Heb.* The men.
[b] *So Sept.; Heb. prefixes* And the chiefs said to them.
[c] *So Sept.; Heb.* they were.
[d] The people...do: *so some Sept. MSS.; Heb. om.*

You told us that you live a long way off, when you are
23 near neighbours. There is a curse upon you for this: for all time you shall provide us with slaves, to chop wood
24 and draw water for the house of my God.' They answered Joshua, 'We were told, sir, that the LORD your God had commanded Moses his servant to give you the whole country and to exterminate all its inhabitants; so because of you we were in terror of our lives, and that is why we
25 did this. We are in your power: do with us whatever
26 you think right and proper.' What he did was this: he saved them from death at the hands of the Israelites, and
27 they did not kill them; but thenceforward he set them to chop wood and draw water for the community and for the altar of the LORD. And to this day they do it at the place which the LORD chose.

✳ This story reports how Joshua and the Israelites were out-manoeuvred – not on the battlefield but in negotiations – by the citizens of Gibeon, who tricked them into a treaty. It tells first of the plot and the conclusion of the agreement (verses 3–15) and second of the discovery of the fraud and Israel's decision to honour the treaty but to reduce the Gibeonites to the status of slaves (verses 16–27*a*). The account concludes with an aetiology (verse 27*b*). The Gibeonites used the Israelites' faithfulness to their promises and their fear of breaking an oath to ensure their own safety, but in the end Joshua and his people had the upper hand.

The motif of trickery – and of the trickster who was tricked – is a common one in folk literature, and the tone of the folk-tale is strong here. There are several implausible elements, including the idea that the Israelites would be fooled by such a simple ruse and the tradition that Gibeon, 'a large place, like a royal city', whose men 'were all good fighters' (10: 2), would beg the invaders for a treaty. Other Old

Testament tales with similar motifs are the narrative of Jacob's deception of his father to win his brother's birthright (Gen. 27), Laban's unsuccessful attempt to trick Jacob out of his rightful share of the flocks and the latter's successful ploy (Gen. 30: 25–43), and the story of the treaty between the sons of Jacob and Shechem, which the former broke in order to take revenge because of the violation of their sister Dinah (Gen. 34).

The tale is an aetiology: it explains why the foreign Gibeonites serve as menials in Israelite worship. But the purpose of the story goes deeper. It is an attempt to reconcile the theological idea that all the previous inhabitants of the promised land were to be killed with the well-known fact that many of them survived. In this regard the account is similar to the story of the rescue of Rahab from Jericho in accordance with the sworn agreement between the prostitute and the Israelite spies (2; 6: 17, 22–5; see comments on 6: 17–19). The major results of the encounter with the Gibeonites seem well founded historically: foreigners in connection with the Israelite cult were known, and there is further evidence of a peaceful agreement with Gibeon. According to 2 Sam. 21: 1–11, consultation of the LORD revealed that a famine in the time of David was the result of Saul's attempt 'to exterminate' the Gibeonites, who are described as foreigners whom the Israelites 'had sworn that they would spare'. (The famine ended when David acceded to the Gibeonites' request that seven of Saul's descendants be killed.)

A careful reading of this story reveals evidence that it is the work of several hands. The language of the Deuteronomistic editor can be seen in verses 9–10, 24–5 (which depend upon Deut. 20: 10–18), and 27*b* (cp. Deut. 12: 5). Furthermore, there are inconsistencies and duplicates in the remaining material which indicate diverse older traditions. Were all the Gibeonites made slaves (verses 21, 27) or only some of them (verse 23)? Where, precisely, did they serve, *for the community* (verse 21), *for the house of my God* (verse 23), or *for the community and for the altar of the LORD* (verse 27 a)? But most of the difficulties have to do with the parties to the treaty. Did one city (so most of the story) or four cities (see verse 17) sue for peace? Who acted for Israel, 'the chiefs' (verses 18-21 and the Septuagint of verse 14), 'the men' (the Hebrew of verse 14), 'the man of Israel' (the Hebrew of verses 6 b, 7 a), or Joshua (verses 6 a, 8, 24-7)? In view of these variations, some scholars have seen here the combination of two independent traditions, one in which Israel made the agreement and another in which Joshua spoke for the people. This view is less likely than the more widely held opinion that an original tradition (in which Joshua did not appear) has been supplemented and revised.

Since the entire story is based on the premise that the native Palestinians had to find some means of escaping extermination, it is clear that the idea of total destruction is not the invention of the Deuteronomistic historian but stems from the ancient holy-war tradition.

3. *Gibeon* has now been identified conclusively with el-Jīb, a site on the central mountain range, about 13 kilometres (8 miles) north-west of Jerusalem, looking down toward the coastal plain (see Maps 1, 3, 4, 6). A recent American archaeological expedition discovered a number of jar handles, probably from the city's prosperous wine industry, inscribed with the name of the city. A relatively large city with strong defences stood on the site during most periods from about 3000 B.C. to the first century B.C. Unfortunately, no remains from the period of the conquest have been discovered except two tombs. Gibeon figures significantly in the history of Israel. It is listed as one of the cities of the tribe of Benjamin (18: 25ff.) and named as one of the Levitical cities (21: 17; see comments on 21: 9-42). It was the scene of battles in the time of David (2 Sam. 2: 12-16; 20: 4-13); the incident involving David, the Gibeonites and the descendants of Saul (2 Sam. 21: 1-11) has been mentioned above. Furthermore, a very important sanctuary was located there. Before he built

the temple in Jerusalem, Solomon offered huge sacrifices at Gibeon, 'for that was the chief hill-shrine', and the LORD appeared to him there and granted his prayer for wisdom (1 Kings 3: 4–15).

6. *treaty*: here appropriately translates the word (*berīt*), usually 'covenant'. A *berīt* could be established by oath between God and men (e.g. ch. 24), between individuals (e.g. David and Jonathan, 1 Sam. 18: 3), or between nations (e.g. Solomon and King Hiram of Tyre, 1 Kings 5: 12). The language here (*grant us a treaty*) clearly indicates that the Gibeonites wish to become vassals of Israel. Such relationships were common in ancient Near Eastern treaties. The contents of the agreement are not specified, but it would have included peace between the parties (cp. verse 15). The mutual defence implied in Joshua's campaign against Gibeon's attackers (10: 1–15) is consistent with ancient vassal treaties.

7. *Hivites*: the Septuagint reads 'Horites', probably meaning the Hurrians (see note on 3: 10). In 2 Sam. 21: 2, on the other hand, the Gibeonites are referred to as 'a remnant of Amorite stock'.

in our neighbourhood: the ruse of the Gibeonites and this response by the Israelites presuppose the idea that no peace could be made with the natives of the land. The reasons for this idea were religious: Canaanite religion was perceived as a threat to that of Israel, and indeed it was, as, for example, the stories of the struggle between Elijah and the followers of the god Baal show (cp. 1 Kings 18–19).

8. *We are your slaves* (cp. verse 11): the expression is a common polite greeting, but in the context it is given special significance. In requesting a treaty the Gibeonites profess to be subservient to Israel, and in the end that is their fate.

10. *Sihon...and Og*: see Num. 21: 21–35; Deut. 2: 26 – 3: 17, and the comments on 12: 1–6.

14. *accepted...provisions*: though the meal consisted of 'nothing but dry and mouldy bread' (verse 5), it was part of the ritual of sealing the agreement (cp. Exod. 18: 12; Gen. 31: 54).

15. This verse consists of the formal legal language involved in consummating a covenant. *received them peaceably*: literally, 'established peace with them'. This 'peace' (*shālōm*) meant more than the absence of hostility; it included seeking the welfare of the other. The *oath* was a conditional self-curse: if one failed to keep one's promise it was believed that the curse became effective.

17. *third day*: according to 10: 9, the Israelites were able to march to Gibeon in a single night. The four cities mentioned here are listed with those of the tribe of Benjamin (18: 24ff.). On *Kiriath-jearim* see Gazetteer.

21. As the N.E.B. footnotes indicate, the verse presents several textual problems. Most of these difficulties seem to have resulted from the ambiguity concerning who was acting for Israel.

23. *house of my God*: where was this sanctuary, and 'the altar of the LORD' mentioned in verse 27*a*? The phrase may be a late gloss on the text referring to the temple in Jerusalem, the place may be the 'chief hill-shrine' at Gibeon (1 Kings 3: 4; see comments on verse 3), or it may have reference to a sanctuary at Gilgal.

27. *to this day*: see the note on 4: 9. *the place which the LORD chose*: that is, the temple in Jerusalem which eventually will be designated as the only legitimate place of worship. ✻

THE DEFEAT OF THE FIVE-KING COALITION

10 When Adoni-zedek king of Jerusalem heard that Joshua had captured Ai and destroyed it (for Joshua had dealt with Ai and her king as he had dealt with Jericho and her king), and that the inhabitants of Gibeon had made their peace with Israel and were living among them, 2 he was[a] greatly alarmed; for Gibeon was a large place, like a royal city: it was larger than Ai, and its men were

[a] *So Pesh.; Heb.* they were.

all good fighters. So Adoni-zedek king of Jerusalem sent 3
to Hoham king of Hebron, Piram king of Jarmuth,
Japhia king of Lachish, and Debir king of Eglon, and
said, 'Come up and help me, and we will attack the 4
Gibeonites, because they have made their peace with
Joshua and the Israelites.' So the five Amorite kings, the 5
kings of Jerusalem, Hebron, Jarmuth, Lachish, and Eglon,
joined forces and advanced to take up their positions for
the attack on Gibeon. But the men of Gibeon sent this 6
message to Joshua in the camp at Gilgal: 'We are your
slaves, do not abandon us, come quickly to our relief.
All the Amorite kings in the hill-country have joined
forces against us; come and help us.' So Joshua went up 7
from Gilgal with all his forces and all his fighting men.
The LORD said to Joshua, 'Do not be afraid of them; I 8
have delivered them into your hands, and not a man will
be able to stand against you.' Joshua came upon them 9
suddenly, after marching all night from Gilgal. The 10
LORD threw them into confusion before the Israelites, and
Joshua defeated them utterly in Gibeon; he pursued them
down the pass of Beth-horon and kept up the slaughter
as far as Azekah and Makkedah. As they were fleeing from 11
Israel down the pass, the LORD hurled great hailstones
at them out of the sky all the way to Azekah: more died
from the hailstones than the Israelites slew by the sword.

On that day when the LORD delivered the Amorites 12
into the hands of Israel, Joshua spoke with the LORD, and
he said in the presence of Israel:

> Stand still, O Sun, in Gibeon;
> stand, Moon, in the Vale of Aijalon.

13 So the sun stood still and the moon halted until a nation
had taken vengeance on its enemies, as indeed is written
in the Book of Jashar.[a] The sun stayed in mid heaven and
14 made no haste to set for almost a whole day. Never before
or since has there been such a day as this day on which the
LORD listened to the voice of a man; for the LORD fought
15 for Israel. So Joshua and all the Israelites returned to the
camp at Gilgal.

✡ This entire chapter (10: 1–43) is presented as the history of Joshua's conquest of the region south of Gibeon, in particular, the southern hill country and the Shephelah. There are four logical divisions in the account (verses 1–15; 16–27; 28–39; 40–3), corresponding in general to the literary history of the material. Separate traditions have been combined and edited to comprise the narrative of the southern campaigns.

This first unit is linked to the account of the treaty with the Gibeonites in 9: 3–27. It is a story of holy warfare (see comments on ch. 6, pp. 54–5). When the king of Jerusalem learns that his neighbours to the north have made their peace with Israel he forms a coalition of five royal cities to attack Gibeon. But Joshua responds to the call for aid, routs the attackers and – through the aid of miracles – thoroughly defeats them. The next section (verses 16–27) stands in the present context as the conclusion, accounting for the death of the five kings.

There are indications that even this short battle narrative had a complex history of transmission. The writer explicitly states that he has drawn upon another work, 'the Book of Jashar' (verse 13, see comment). Two different escape routes are mentioned, in verse 10*b* and verse 11*a*; the latter is the logical road down from the region of Gibeon. Furthermore, the LORD intervened three times, by throwing the enemy 'into confusion' (verse 10), by hurling 'hailstones' (verse 11), and by lengthening the day (verses 13–14). These last facts

[*a*] *Or* the Book of the Upright.

may be explained as distinct stages in the battle, or as the result of the combination of traditions. More significant is the fact that much of this story is duplicated in Judg. 1: 4ff. There three of the cities listed are said to have been taken by the tribe of Judah.

1. *Adoni-zedek*: according to Judg. 1: 5–7 and the Septuagint of this verse, the king of Jerusalem was 'Adoni-bezek'. The variation is a simple one, so it seems most likely that the texts have in mind the same king. Judg 1: 8 reports that 'The men of Judah' captured Jerusalem and burned it, but Judg. 1: 21 states that 'the Benjamites' could not drive out the inhabitants of the city, so they lived there with them. (See comments on 15: 6–11; 18: 25–8.)

3. According to 14: 6–15 and 15: 13–19, *Hebron* was given to Caleb. On the location and history of Hebron, see notes on 14: 14–15. *Jarmuth* is identified with Khirbet el-Yarmūk, *Lachish* with Tell ed-Duweir, and *Eglon* probably is Tell el-Ḥesī. (For the location of all five cities see Map 1.) In 10: 38 and elsewhere, *Debir* – which occurs here as the name of the king of Eglon – is the name of a city. The place name probably was mistakenly given here as a personal name.

5. The siege of Gibeon would have been calculated both to cut off Israel's advance into the hill-country and to punish those who allied themselves with the invaders.

8. The language of the LORD's speech to Joshua is a sort of formula, corresponding to the necessary consultation of the deity before the holy warfare could begin (cp. 8: 1). As in the report of the second attack on Ai (8: 1–29), there is no mention of the presence of the Ark.

10. *confusion*: the usual panic of the LORD's enemies in the holy war. *the pass of Beth-horon*, the usual entrance to the hill-country, is slightly north-west of Gibeon (see Maps 1, 4, and 6). *Azekah* (cp. verse 11) is much further to the south, and *Makkedah* cannot be identified with certainty.

11. *great hailstones*: a second miracle occurs; the LORD intervenes from heaven (cp. Judg. 5: 19–21).

12–14. The writer includes and interprets a poetic couplet from the *Book of Jashar*. Since this book is cited again as the source of the lament over Saul and Jonathan (2 Sam. 1: 17–27) it seems likely that it was an ancient collection of heroic poetry. The poetry is but loosely related to its context. The original poem seems to have been only verse 12 b, a prayer addressed to the sun and the moon, but introduced here as Joshua's prayer to the LORD. While verse 13 a also could be read as poetic lines – and is so treated in the Hebrew text – it appears to be a very early interpretation of the preceding couplet, explaining how the prayer was answered. Verse 13 b is a further, even more specific, interpretation of the poem, and in verse 14 the writer stands in awe of the LORD and of the greatness of Joshua, whose prayer was answered. The successive interpretations of the original lines take the poetry quite literally: the sun and the moon (ignored in 13 b) stopped in the heavens in order to provide enough light for the completion of the battle. It is quite possible that the interpreters, in stressing the intervention of the LORD, have changed the original meaning of the couplet. There are strong echoes of myth in the poem. The heavenly bodies were of great importance in the religions of Israel's neighbours, and in the original lines the prayer to the moon is equally as important as the address to the sun. It seems quite possible, as some scholars have argued recently, that the setting of the poem is the practice of astrology or astronomy and the request for a favourable sign.

15. In view of the next section (verses 16–27) in which Joshua and his army are still in pursuit of the enemy, the return to the camp at Gilgal makes little sense. The verse does not appear in the Septuagint. *

THE EXECUTION OF THE FIVE KINGS

16 The five kings fled and hid themselves in a cave at
17 Makkedah, and Joshua was told that they had been found
18 hidden in this cave. Joshua replied, 'Roll some great

stones to the mouth of the cave and post men there to
keep watch over the kings. But you must not stay; keep 19
up the pursuit, attack your enemies from the rear and do
not let them reach their cities; the LORD your God has
delivered them into your hands.' When Joshua and the 20
Israelites had finished the work of slaughter and all had
been put to the sword – except a few survivors who
escaped and entered the fortified cities – the whole army 21
rejoined*a* Joshua at Makkedah in peace; not a man*b* of the
Israelites suffered so much as a scratch on his tongue. Then 22
Joshua said, 'Open the mouth of the cave, and bring me
out those five kings.' They did so; they brought the 23
five kings out of the cave, the kings of Jerusalem, Hebron,
Jarmuth, Lachish, and Eglon. When they had brought 24
them to Joshua, he summoned all the Israelites and said
to the commanders of the troops who had served with
him, 'Come forward and put your feet on the necks of
these kings.' So they came forward and put their feet
on their necks. Joshua said to them, 'Do not be fearful 25
or dismayed; be strong and resolute; for the LORD will
do this to every enemy you fight against.' And he struck 26
down the kings and slew them; then he hung their bodies
on five trees, where they remained hanging till evening.
At sunset, on Joshua's orders they took them down from 27
the trees and threw them into the cave in which they had
hidden; they piled great stones against its mouth, and
there the stones are to this day.*c*

[a] *So Sept.; Heb. adds* at the camp.
[b] *So Sept.; Heb.* not for a man.
[c] and there...day: *or* on this very day.

✵ These verses assume the coalition of the five cities against Gibeon (verses 1–15), and describe how the leaders were captured and killed. While the Israelites were pursuing their army, the kings were trapped in a cave at Makkedah and later executed. The story is an aetiology, explicitly the explanation of the origin of the pile of stones at the mouth of the cave as the tomb of five of Israel's enemies. However, there are other motifs, leading some commentators to suggest that the original aetiology explained the five remarkable trees in Makkedah, and that while one version of the tradition remembered that Joshua hanged the kings on the trees, another account originally told of their suffocation in the cave.

It should be noted that neither this story nor the preceding unit reports attacks on the cities of the coalition; only the armies and the kings were killed. The next section (verses 28–39) will report the destruction of some of the cities.

16. *Makkedah*, which cannot be located with certainty, must have been in the region of Lachish (see comment on verse 31). The city was not part of the coalition; the kings were unable to escape to their 'fortified cities' (cp. verse 20).

19–21. In contrast to the note in verse 15, the battle continues and Joshua seems to have established a camp at Makkedah.

21. *not a man of the Israelites suffered so much as a scratch on his tongue*: the text presents some difficulties, with some variations in the Septuagint, probably because of the obscurity of the Hebrew idiom. Read perhaps, 'not a man wagged his tongue against the people of Israel'.

24. The public humiliation of the kings before their execution is a ritual of submission. By placing their feet on the necks of the kings, the *commanders of the troops* – on behalf of the people – take control over them and what is theirs. Such rituals are mentioned poetically in Deut. 33: 29 and in Ps. 110: 1:

> The LORD said to my lord,
> 'You shall sit at my right hand
> when I make your enemies the footstool under your feet.'

25. The submission of the five kings is taken as assurance that all Israel's enemies will be defeated.

26–7. On the removal of the bodies *At sunset*, see Deut. 21: 22–3 and the comments on 8: 29. On the formula, *to this day*, see the note on 4: 9. ✶

THE SOUTHERN CAMPAIGN

On that same day, Joshua captured Makkedah and put 28 both king and people to the sword, destroying both them and every living thing in the city. He left no survivor, and he dealt with the king of Makkedah as he had dealt with the king of Jericho. Then Joshua and all the Israelites 29 marched on from Makkedah to Libnah and attacked it. The LORD delivered the city and its king to the Israelites, 30 and they put its people and every living thing in it to the sword; they left no survivor there, and dealt with its king as they had dealt with the king of Jericho. From 31 Libnah Joshua and all the Israelites marched on to Lachish, took up their positions and attacked it. The LORD delivered 32 Lachish into their hands; they took it on the second day and put every living thing in it to the sword, as they had done at Libnah.

Meanwhile Horam king of Gezer had advanced to the 33 relief of Lachish; but Joshua struck them down, both king and people, and not a man of them survived. Then 34 Joshua and all the Israelites marched on from Lachish to Eglon, took up their positions and attacked it; that same 35 day they captured it and put its inhabitants to the sword, destroying every living thing in it as they had done at Lachish. From Eglon Joshua and all the Israelites ad- 36 vanced to Hebron and attacked it. They captured it and 37

put its king to the sword together with every living thing
in it and in all its villages; as at Eglon, he left no survivor,
38 destroying it and every living thing in it. Then Joshua
and all the Israelites wheeled round towards Debir and
39 attacked it. They captured the city with its king, and all
its villages, put them to the sword and destroyed every
living thing; they left no survivor. They dealt with
Debir and its king as they had dealt with Hebron and
with Libnah and its king.

✳ The material in this section is quite different from any
which has preceded it in the book of Joshua. There are no
detailed stories of battles, aetiological tales, or general descriptions of the conquered territory. This account of the
campaign against the cities of the south quickly lists one
battle after another, adding only the briefest note to establish
that each conflict was a holy war. The foundation for the
account appears to be a traditional itinerary which noted the
sequence of the victories.

While the report of these victories is linked to the remainder
of ch. 10 by the starting-point at Makkedah and the general
overlapping of this territory and that of the five-king coalition,
there are several distinctive features which indicate that we
have here a tradition which once circulated independently.
Some, but not all, of the cities of the coalition were attacked:
Jerusalem and Jarmuth do not appear in the list of victories.
(On the problem of the capture of Jerusalem, see comments
on 10: 1. The most reliable account of the acquisition of the
city is found in 2 Sam. 5: 6–9, which indicates that Jerusalem
retained its independence until the time of David.) Furthermore, other cities not in the coalition were captured: Makkedah, Libnah and Debir.

According to this account, Joshua captured six cities and
killed their inhabitants. The king and army of a seventh city,
Gezer, were annihilated when they came to the relief of

Lachish. All six cities are listed in the territory of the tribe of Judah (cp. 15: 39–54), Makkedah, Libnah, Lachish and Eglon in the Shephelah; Hebron and Debir in the hill-country. (On the location and identification of these cities, see Map 1 and the Gazetteer.) Again Gezer is distinctive, appearing in the boundary list of Joseph (16: 3). Thus we have before us a tradition from the tribe of Judah, in contrast to the pre-dominance of Benjamite traditions up to this point.

28. *Makkedah*: see comment on verse 16. *the king* does not occur in the Septuagint. *the king of Jericho* had not been mentioned in the story of the destruction of the city (ch. 6).

29. *Libnah* is listed as one of the Levitical cities (see comments on ch. 21 and Map 6).

31. The excavation of *Lachish* (Tell ed-Duweir) in 1932–8 revealed that the Late Bronze Age city was destroyed by fire about 1220 B.C. and then re-occupied about 900 B.C. While the date of the destruction coincides with the best estimate of the time of the conquest, there can be no assurance that the invading Israelites were responsible for that particular fire.

33. The report in 16: 10 (see comment and cp. Judg. 1: 29) that the tribe of Joseph was unable to 'drive out the Canaanites who lived in Gezer' is consistent with the fact that this account does not mention the capture and destruction of the city. According to 1 Kings 9: 15–16, Solomon rebuilt Gezer, which had been burnt 'to the ground' by Pharaoh, king of Egypt.

36. The divergent traditions concerning the capture of *Hebron* have been mentioned already in connection with 10: 3 (see also Judg. 1: 9ff., 20 and the comments on 14: 14–15).

38. The location of *Debir* is disputed; see the comment on 15: 16. Like Hebron, the capture of Debir is attributed to Joshua in this context and elsewhere to the clan of Caleb (15: 13–19) and to the tribe of Judah in general (Judg. 1: 11ff.). Further confusion is created by the fact that the name of the city appears in 10: 3 as the name of the king of Eglon. ✳

CONQUERED LANDS

40 So Joshua massacred the population of the whole region
– the hill-country, the Negeb, the Shephelah, the watersheds – and all their kings. He left no survivor, destroying
everything that drew breath, as the LORD the God of
41 Israel had commanded. Joshua carried the slaughter from
Kadesh-barnea to Gaza, over the whole land of Goshen
42 and as far as Gibeon. All these kings he captured at the
same time, and their country with them, for the LORD
43 the God of Israel fought for Israel. And Joshua returned
with all the Israelites to the camp at Gilgal.

✷ The Deuteronomistic editor again (cp. 9: 1–2; 11: 16–23)
summarizes the events and in doing so includes more than
had been reported in the individual stories. The general statement is meant to encompass all the conquests reported in
chs. 2–10, but it includes more. It has in mind all – or virtually
all – the territory in Palestine south of Gibeon (verse 41).

40. *the whole region*: literally, 'all the land'. The writer
describes the conquered land in terms of topographical regions.

41. The editor now draws a line sweeping from south to
north across the land captured, from *Kadesh-barnea* in the
southern Negeb (see Map 1 and the Gazetteer) to *Gaza*, a
Philistine city on the coastal plain, *over the whole land of Goshen*
and as far north as *Gibeon*. Elsewhere (13: 3) Gaza is included
among the unconquered cities, but Judg. 1: 18 reports that
the tribe of Judah took the city and its territory. Gaza must
be listed here to give the westward limit of the southern
conquests. The land of Goshen mentioned here (and in
11: 16) cannot be located except generally in the southern
part of Palestine. ✷

THE NORTHERN CAMPAIGN

When Jabin king of Hazor heard of all this, he sent to **11**
Jobab king of Madon, to the kings of Shimron and
Akshaph, to the northern kings in the hill-country, in 2
the Arabah opposite*a* Kinnereth, in the Shephelah, and
in the district of Dor on the west, the Canaanites to the 3
east and the west, the Amorites, Hittites, Perizzites, and
Jebusites in the hill-country, and the Hivites below
Hermon in the land of Mizpah. They took the field with 4
all their forces, a great horde countless as the grains of
sand on the sea-shore, among them a great number of
horses and chariots. All these kings made common cause, 5
and came and encamped at the waters of Merom to fight
against Israel. The LORD said to Joshua, 'Do not be afraid 6
of them, for at this time tomorrow I shall deliver them to
Israel all dead men; you shall hamstring their horses and
burn their chariots.' So Joshua and his army surprised 7
them by the waters of Merom and fell upon them. The 8
LORD delivered them into the hands of Israel; they struck
them down and pursued them as far as Greater Sidon,
Misrephoth on the west, and the Vale of Mizpah on the
east. They struck them down until not a man was left
alive. Joshua dealt with them as the LORD had com- 9
manded: he hamstrung their horses and burnt their
chariots.

At this point Joshua turned his forces against Hazor, 10
formerly the head of all these kingdoms. He captured the
city and put its king to death with the sword. They killed 11
every living thing in it and wiped them all out; they

[a] *So Sept.; Heb.* south of.

spared nothing that drew breath, and Hazor itself they
12 destroyed by fire. So Joshua captured these kings and their
cities and put them to the sword, destroying them all, as
13 Moses the servant of the LORD had commanded. The
cities whose ruined mounds are still standing were not
burnt by the Israelites; it was Hazor alone that Joshua
14 burnt. The Israelites plundered all these cities and kept
for themselves the cattle and any other spoil they took;
but they put every living soul to the sword until they
had destroyed every one; they did not leave alive any
15 one that drew breath. The LORD laid his commands on
his servant Moses, and Moses laid these same commands
on Joshua, and Joshua carried them out. Not one of the
commands laid on Moses by the LORD did he leave
unfulfilled.

* The previous chapter had reached the logical conclusion
of the events set into motion in ch. 2: Joshua and Israel had
taken southern Palestine. This report of victory in the north
has something of the appearance of an appendix: it must have
circulated independently, probably as the traditions of one or
more northern tribes, before it was made a part of the account
of the conquest by all Israel under Joshua. The transition is
abrupt, the only link with the preceding narrative being the
note that 'Jabin king of Hazor heard of all this', i.e. of Israel's
victories.

Nevertheless, in some ways this story parallels that of the
Judaean campaign in ch. 10. In response to Israel's success,
one king forms a coalition of several cities, but again Joshua
takes the offensive, defeating the armies, executing the kings
and then attacking their cities. There are two main parts to
the story: (1) the account of the formation of the coalition
and its defeat at 'the waters of Merom' (verses 1–9), and
(2) the campaign against the cities with a summary of the

victories (verses 10–15). All in all, the traditions concerning
the settlement of the north in general and Galilee in particular
are meagre, but those preserved here seem to rest upon good
historical foundations, probably – as some commentators have
suggested – concerning the expansion of the tribe of Naphtali
into the territory of Hazor.

1. *Jabin* appears again in the period of the Judges as 'the
Canaanite king, who ruled in Hazor' (Judg. 4: 1; cp. Judg.
4: 23–4) but that notice should not be taken as a parallel
tradition concerning the capture of his city. In Judg. 4–5 the
primary tradition deals with the victory over Sisera.

Hazor (Tell el-Qedaḥ, see Map 1), granted to the northern-
most tribe of Naphtali (19: 36), is located approximately
8 kilometres (5 miles) south-west of Lake Huleh. The archaeological excavation of the site (1955–8) has demonstrated that
it was a huge city, well qualified to be 'the head of all these
kingdoms' (verse 10). In the Late Bronze Age a lower city
surrounded by earthwork defences covered about 80 hectares
(200 acres); inside, the citadel on the mound covered some
10 hectares (25 acres). The city was destroyed in the middle of
the thirteenth century B.C., a time which corresponds generally
to the best estimate of the period of the Israelite conquest. The
excavators found evidence of two settlements on the mound
before the city was rebuilt by Solomon (1 Kings 9: 15).

The other three cities are south of Hazor. *Madon* is identified
with Khirbet Midyan just west of the Sea of Galilee (see
Map 1); neither *Shimron* (see comments on 12: 20 and Map 1)
nor *Akshaph* (see Map 1 and the Gazetteer) can be identified
with certainty.

2. The enumeration of the participants in the coalition
begins very specifically and becomes progressively vaguer
and broader. The previous verse had given the kings of two
cities by name and listed two more cities; now all *the
northern kings* are mentioned by region only. *Kinnereth* is
the Sea of Galilee and *the district of Dor* seems to have been on
the coast of the Mediterranean (see the note on 12: 23).

3. This familiar listing of the pre-Israelite inhabitants of Palestine is different from previous ones in the book of Joshua (see comments on 3: 10) in that it places the groups in general areas. The reference to the *Jebusites* in a list of northerners is unusual, since they are mentioned elsewhere only with reference to the city of Jerusalem or in the lists of the people of the entire country. This fact supports the impression that the stereotyped enumeration of all the previous inhabitants has been adapted for this specific story.

5. The *waters of Merom* have been associated with the Wadi Meirūn which flows into the Sea of Galilee. The region does not provide sufficient open terrain for chariots to be effective. This situation suggests the note in Judg. 1: 19: 'The LORD was with Judah and they occupied the hill-country, but they could not drive out the inhabitants of the Vale because they had chariots of iron.'

6. Where was Joshua when he received the LORD's instructions? The text does not say but seems to assume that the camp had remained in Gilgal (cp. 14: 6). The assurance to Joshua (6a) is the typical formula which precedes the holy war (cp. 10: 8, etc.). The second half of the verse is a command, as verse 9 indicates.

7. While the LORD is responsible for the success, the victory is accomplished by means of tactics – the selection of the battlefield and the element of surprise – and not through a miracle.

8. The pursuit of the fleeing enemy is a consistent element in the holy war accounts. The army fled to the north. *Greater Sidon* is the city on the coast of Lebanon, *Misrephoth* is at the western end of the Palestinian frontier, and the *Vale of Mizpah* must be at the other end of the natural boundary, below Mount Hermon (cp. verse 3).

12. *Moses the servant of the LORD*: see the comments on 1: 2.

13. The previous verses (10–12) are clarified: *Hazor*, its king and inhabitants, had been destroyed, along with the kings and people of the other cities. But no other cities were

destroyed. Read more literally: 'But all the cities which are standing on their mounds, Israel did not burn them.'

14. The 'solemn ban' (see comments on 6: 17–19) is extended only to the inhabitants; this is not the first occasion when an exception was made to allow the taking of *spoil* (cp. 8: 26–7).

15. The wars of conquest have reached a successful conclusion because of the perfect obedience of Joshua to the commandments transmitted through Moses. The faithfulness of the chosen leader is matched by the LORD's fulfilment of his promises: 'Not a word of the LORD's promises to the house of Israel went unfulfilled; they all came true' (21: 45). ✶

A SUMMARY OF JOSHUA'S CONQUESTS

And so Joshua took the whole country, the hill-country, all the Negeb, all the land of Goshen, the Shephelah, the Arabah, and the Israelite hill-country with the adjoining lowlands. His conquests extended from the bare mountain which leads up to Seir as far as Baal-gad in the Vale of Lebanon under Mount Hermon. He took prisoner all their kings, struck them down and put them to death. It was a long war that he fought against all these kingdoms. Except for the Hivites who lived in Gibeon, not one of their cities came to terms with the Israelites; all were taken by storm. It was the LORD's purpose that they should offer an obstinate resistance to the Israelites in battle, and that thus they should be annihilated without mercy and utterly destroyed,[a] as the LORD had commanded Moses.

It was then that Joshua proceeded to wipe out the

[a] offer...destroyed: *or* obstinately engage the Israelites in battle so that they should annihilate them without mercy, only that he might destroy them...

Anakim from the hill-country, from Hebron, Debir, Anab, all the hill-country of Judah and all the hill-country of Israel, destroying both them and their cities.

22 No Anakim were left in the land taken by the Israelites; they survived only in Gaza, Gath, and Ashdod.

23 Thus Joshua took the whole country, fulfilling all the commands that the LORD had laid on Moses; he assigned it as Israel's patrimony, allotting to each tribe its share; and the land was at peace.

✵ Joshua's territorial conquests are summarized. Note that this summary implies a more complete conquest of the territory west of the Jordan than the preceding narratives actually support. The claim that Joshua 'took the whole country' is further qualified by data which the Deuteronomistic editor will introduce later. See especially the list of unconquered territories (13: 1–6) and the lists of unconquered cities (15: 63; 16: 10; 17: 11–13 and Judg. 1: 21, 27–35).

16. This verse, which surveys the conquered territory according to its natural geographical divisions, is somewhat redundant. The geographical divisions of Judah which are listed in the first part of the verse – *the hill-country, all the Negeb, all the land of Goshen, the Shephelah* – would be included in the latter part of the verse which is a more general survey of the whole territory west of the Jordan – *the Arabah, and the Israelite hill-country with the adjoining lowlands* (i.e. the Shephelah). Note, on the other hand, that the coastal lands along the Mediterranean are not mentioned in either case.

17. *the bare mountain* (or 'Mount Halak') *which leads up to Seir* and *Baal-gad* mark respectively the southern and northern limits of the conquered territory. Elsewhere in the Old Testament, Israel's territorial limits are often said to have extended from Beersheba to Dan (Judg. 20: 1; 1 Chron. 21: 2; see the note on Josh. 1: 4) which is a slightly more modest, but not essentially different, claim.

20. This verse is textually problematic, but its point is clear enough. God ordained that the earlier inhabitants of the promised land would resist Israel so that they could be annihilated.

21–2. It would appear from this passage that the *Anakim* were spread throughout *the hill-country* and that Joshua wiped them all out except for a few who survived in the three Philistine cities of *Gaza, Gath, and Ashdod*. However, these Anakim will appear again in the passages concerning the Calebites (14: 6–15; 15: 13–19), where their presence will be confined primarily to Hebron and their defeat attributed to Caleb. ✶

THE KINGS WHOM ISRAEL SLEW: SIHON AND OG

These are the names of the kings of the land whom the **12** Israelites slew, and whose territory they occupied beyond the Jordan towards the sunrise from the gorge of the Arnon as far as Mount Hermon and all the Arabah on the east. Sihon the Amorite king who lived in Heshbon: 2 his rule extended from Aroer, which is on the edge of the gorge of the Arnon, along the middle of the gorge and over half Gilead as far as the gorge of the Jabbok, the Ammonite frontier; along the Arabah as far as the eastern 3 side of the Sea of Kinnereth and as far as the eastern side of the Sea of the Arabah, the Dead Sea, by the road to Beth-jeshimoth and from Teman under the watershed of Pisgah. Og*a* king of Bashan, one of the survivors of 4 the Rephaim, who lived in Ashtaroth and Edrei: he ruled 5 over Mount Hermon, Salcah, all Bashan as far as the Geshurite and Maacathite borders, and half Gilead as far as*b* the boundary of Sihon king of Heshbon. Moses the 6

[*a*] So Sept.; *Heb.* the boundary of Og.
[*b*] as far as: *so Luc. Sept.; Heb. om.*

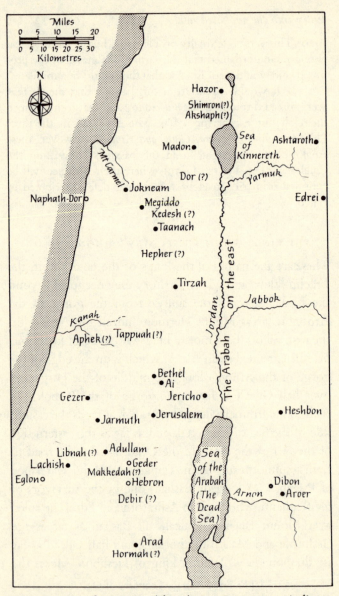

2. Summary of conquests (ch. 12). See Gazetteer. ● indicates that the site can be established fairly conclusively. ○ indicates that the site can be established with some probability. (?) indicates that the general vicinity can be established.

servant of the LORD put them to death, he and the Israelites, and he gave their land to the Reubenites, the Gadites, and half the tribe of Manasseh, as their possession

* The summary of Israel's territorial conquests west of the Jordan is followed now by a list of the kings slain during the process of the conquests – including Sihon and Og, whose kingdoms lay east of the Jordan and whose defeat had occurred under Moses' leadership. These two kings have already been mentioned (2: 10; 9: 10). An account of their defeat is provided in Num. 21: 21–35 and reviewed in Deut. 2: 26 – 3: 11.

1. The southern and northern limits of the conquered territory west of the Jordan have been defined in 11: 17 (see also 12: 7). The corresponding limits east of the Jordan are defined here: *the gorge of the Arnon* in the south and *Mount Hermon* (the southernmost spur of the Anti-Lebanon range) in the north.

2–3. *Heshbon*, Sihon's capital city, is currently (1973) being excavated by archaeologists. Thus far, however, no architectural remains have been uncovered which date earlier than the seventh century B.C. The phrase *from Aroer, which is on the edge of the gorge of the Arnon, along the middle of the gorge* is probably a corruption of the descriptive formula which appears in three corresponding passages: 'from Aroer which is by the edge of the gorge of the Arnon, and the city which is in the middle of the gorge' (Deut. 2: 36; Josh. 13: 9; 2 Sam. 24: 5). *Aroer* was located on the northern edge of the Arnon, near the point where the king's highway crossed in ancient times (Num. 20: 17; 21: 22). Archaeological excavations at the site (1964–5) have uncovered the remains of an Early Bronze Age fortress which apparently was restored and re-used during the Iron Age. The reference to 'the city in the middle of the gorge' is, on the other hand, topographically problematic. There is little justification for the attempt on the part of the N.E.B. translators to ease this problem by rendering the phrase: 'and the level land half-way along the gorge' (13:9).

The river *Jabbok* bisects the mountainous territory of Gilead and apparently served as the boundary between the kingdoms of Sihon and Og (see verse 5). It could hardly have served as the boundary along the Ammonite frontier, however, as verse 2 seems to imply. The account probably intends to suggest that Sihon's realm of authority extended as far north as the Jabbok (see Judg. 11: 22) and as far east as the Ammonite frontier. Sihon is said to have controlled the Arabah on the eastern side of the Jordan as well, as far north as the Sea of Kinnereth (Galilee), and as far south as the north-eastern shore of the Dead Sea. *Teman* means 'south' or 'southern' and probably should be translated accordingly in this passage – i.e. Sihon's kingdom extended 'southward beneath the watershed of Pisgah'.

4. *the Rephaim*, according to Palestinian folklore, were a people of giant stature who had inhabited Bashan in times past. Bashan is in fact called 'the land of the Rephaim' in Deut. 3: 13. Deut. 3: 11 reports that Og's sarcophagus of basalt was nearly 4 metres long and, roughly, 2 metres wide (14 feet by 6 feet)! Gen. 14: 5 refers more specifically to the Rephaim of Ashteroth-karnaim, which probably is identical with the *Ashtaroth* of this passage. Ashtaroth is mentioned several times in the Egyptian records. Both Ashtaroth and *Edrei* were located near the tributaries of the river Yarmuk.

5. Og's realm of authority included the remainder of *Gilead* (see verse 2) and all of *Bashan* – i.e. the region of the river Yarmuk and northward. Excluded from his kingdom, however, was the enclave of Geshurites and Maacathites. The relationship between these Geshurites of Bashan and those who inhabited the coastal area south-west of the Judaean Shephelah (see comment on 13: 2-3) is unclear. Absalom's mother was from a village named Geshur in Bashan (2 Sam. 3: 3), and Absalom fled there after the assassination of his half-brother Amnon (2 Sam. 13: 37-8). The Maacathites were among the allies of the Ammonites in their war with David (2 Sam. 10: 6-18; 1 Chron. 19: 6-9).

6. The assignment of the Transjordanian territory to Reuben, Gad, and half the tribe of Manasseh is reported in Num. 32. The Deuteronomistic editor will describe the individual allotments to these tribes below (13: 7-31). *

THE KINGS WHOM ISRAEL SLEW:
THOSE WEST OF THE JORDAN

These are the names of the kings whom Joshua and the 7 Israelites put to death beyond the Jordan to the west, from Baal-gad in the Vale of Lebanon as far as the bare mountain that leads up to Seir. Joshua gave their land to the Israelite tribes to be their possession according to their allotted shares, in the hill-country, the Shephelah, the 8 Arabah, the watersheds, the wilderness, and the Negeb; lands of the Hittites, Amorites, Canaanites, Perizzites, Hivites, and Jebusites. The king of Jericho; the king of 9 Ai which is beside Bethel; the king of Jerusalem; the king 10 of Hebron; the king of Jarmuth; the king of Lachish; the 11, 12 king of Eglon; the king of Gezer; the king of Debir; the 13 king of Geder; the king of Hormah; the king of Arad; 14 the king of Libnah; the king of Adullam; the king of 15, 16 Makkedah; the king of Bethel; the king of Tappuah; the 17 king of Hepher; the king of Aphek; the king of Aphek[a]- 18 in-Sharon; the king of Madon; the king of Hazor; the 19, 20 king of Shimron-meron;[b] the king of Akshaph; the king 21 of Taanach; the king of Megiddo; the king of Kedesh; 22 the king of Jokneam-in-Carmel; the king of Dor in the 23 district of Dor; the king of Gaiam-in-Galillee;[c] the king 24 of Tirzah: thirty-one kings in all, one of each town.

[a] of Aphek: *prob. rdg.; Heb. om.*   [b] *In 11: 1* Shimron.
[c] Gaiam-in-Galilee: *prob. rdg., cp. Sept.; Heb.* nations to Gilgal.

✻ Those kings whose realms of authority lay west of the Jordan are, in contrast to Sihon and Og, simply listed without any further comment. Literally, the paragraph reads: 'The king of Jericho, one; the king of Ai which is beside Bethel, one; the king of Jerusalem, one; etc.' At least half of the cities whose kings are listed here have already appeared in the preceding chapters of Joshua. The defeat of Arad (verse 14) is described in Num. 21: 1–4, and Hormah is mentioned in the same context. Several of the cities appear here for the first and only time in the conquest traditions, however, raising the possibility that the Deuteronomistic editor was utilizing a city list at this point which was independent of the other conquest narratives. One scholar has recently marshalled archaeological evidence which suggests that, if such a list existed, it must have dated from King Solomon's reign.

It is not always possible to locate geographically the cities mentioned in the biblical texts (see the introductory comments to the Gazetteer on p. 189). Map 2 indicates those in ch. 12 which can be located fairly conclusively, those whose location can be established with some degree of probability, and those whose general vicinity can be established.

18. Note that the reading *Aphek-in-Sharon* requires a slight textual emendation which is supported by the Septuagint. This seems preferable to the reading of the Hebrew text which treats *Aphek* and *Sharon* as two different cities. It was necessary to distinguish Aphek-in-Sharon from at least three other Apheks (see Gazetteer).

20. The reverse has occurred in verse 20, where the Septuagint manuscripts incorrectly treat *Shimron-meron* as two separate sites – e.g. Codex Alexandrinus, a fourth-century manuscript of the Septuagint, reads, 'Samron and Marron'. One is tempted to follow the Septuagint at this point, since the name 'Shimron' stands alone in 11: 1. But it seems more likely that the designation 'meron' was introduced into the list of conquered cities secondarily in order to distinguish this Shimron, which apparently was located in the vicinity of the

'waters of Merom' (see 11: 1-5), from Shimron in Zebulon (19: 15).

23. There were at least two villages named *Dor* in ancient Palestine. The most famous one was situated on the Mediterranean coast and served as the nucleus of Solomon's fourth administrative district (see 11: 2 and 1 Kings 4: 11). It is mentioned in the Egyptian texts; the biblical writers referred to it as 'Naphath-Dor', which the N.E.B. translators render *the district of Dor*. But there must have been another Dor situated in the Jezreel valley. Note that Ps. 83: 10 places 'Endor' (i.e. 'The Spring of Dor') in the Jezreel valley – although the N.E.B. translators have emended the text to read otherwise – and the name has been preserved in that of present-day 'En Dor, located just south of Mount Tabor. It is to this latter Dor that this verse refers, and the same is true as we shall see with regard to 17: 11. Dor is listed in both instances among cities which were situated on the northern slopes of Mount Carmel and in the Jezreel valley. It is also evident in both cases that the phrase 'in the district of Dor' has been added to the text secondarily. The resulting redundancy is especially evident in the passage under discussion.

Gaiam-in-Galilee: the N.E.B. translation follows the Septuagint at this point, and identifies Gaiam as a village in Galilee. The Hebrew text makes a more general reference to the 'nations' or 'people' of 'Gilgal'. Little support can be marshalled for either reading. Furthermore, neither Gaiam nor Gilgal can be located geographically. Certainly this Gilgal cannot be equated with the one near Jericho which serves as Israel's camp throughout chs. 5-17. ✳

The division of the land among the tribes

The Deuteronomistic editor has provided us in the first eleven chapters with a series of narratives which relate Joshua's conquests west of the Jordan. Although these narratives taken as a whole do not imply a complete conquest of the land, the editor nevertheless contends at the end that 'Joshua took the whole country, fulfilling all the commands that the LORD had laid on Moses; he assigned it as Israel's patrimony, allotting to each tribe its share; and the land was at peace' (11: 23). Chs. 12–22 are essentially an elaboration of this statement. Specifically, ch. 12 summarizes the conquests on both sides of the Jordan, thus emphasizing that the whole country within certain designated limits was at Israel's mercy. In 13: 1–14 it is contended that even more territory was actually assigned to Israel than Moses and Joshua had conquered, and thus remained to be taken. Beginning with 13: 15 we are provided with a detailed description of the allotments to the various tribes. This description opens with a survey of the allotments east of the Jordan which Moses had already assigned to Reuben, Gad, and half Manasseh (13: 15–33) and concludes with these two-and-a-half tribes returning to take possession of their lands (ch. 22). The lists of refuge and Levitical cities in chs. 20–1 further emphasize the completeness of Israel's possession of the land.

The primary purpose of this second major division of the book of Joshua, which goes into such elaborate geographical detail, is to emphasize that God had designated 'the whole country' as Israel's possession. This would have been a significant point for the first readers of the book of Joshua who were living at a time when Israel's actual possession of the whole country was only a remembrance of the past and a hope for the future (see the discussion of 'Literary problems', pp. 2–10). ✱

THE TERRITORY WHICH REMAINED UNCONQUERED

BY THIS TIME Joshua had become very old, and the **13** LORD said to him, 'You are now a very old man, and much of the country remains to be occupied. The country 2 which remains is this: all the districts of the Philistines and all the Geshurite country (this is reckoned as Canaan- 3 ite territory from Shihor to the east of Egypt as far north as Ekron; and it belongs to the five lords of the Philistines, those of Gaza, Ashdod, Ashkelon, Gath, and Ekron); all the districts of the Avvim on the south; all the Canaanite 4 country from the low-lying land which belongs to the Sidonians as far as Aphek, the Amorite frontier; the land 5 of the Gebalites and all the Lebanon to the east from Baal-gad under Mount Hermon as far as Lebo-hamath. I will drive out in favour of the Israelites all the inhabi- 6 tants of the hill-country from the Lebanon as far as Misrephoth on the west, and all the Sidonians. In the mean time you are to allot all this to the Israelites for their patrimony, as I have commanded you.'

✳ Ch. 13 is essentially a Deuteronomistic composition in which the editor concedes that not all of the territory to be distributed had actually been conquered (verse 1), describes that which remained unconquered (verses 2–6), and reminds the reader that two-and-a-half tribes had already received territorial allotments east of the Jordan (verses 7–14; see 1: 13–14 and 12: 6). The description in verses 1–6 of the country which 'remains to be occupied' has received several secondary glosses during the process of transmission and is difficult to follow geographically. As these verses now stand, three separate areas seem to be indicated: (1) the territory south-west of the Shephelah inhabited by the Philistines,

Geshurites, and Avvites; (2) the Sidonian territory between the Lebanon (not the anti-Lebanon) Mountains and the Mediterranean Sea; and (3) the territory east of the Lebanon Mountains.

2. *all the districts of the Philistines and all the Geshurite country*: the Philistines were a non-Semitic people who entered Palestine (the name is derived from them) in connection with the so-called 'Sea People' known from the Egyptian records. These 'Sea People', apparently after they were displaced from their original homelands in the Aegean area near the end of the Late Bronze Age, ravaged the coasts of Asia Minor and northern Syria, and even attacked Egypt during the reigns of Merneptah and Rameses III. Three of the five Philistine cities – Ashdod, Ashkelon, and Gaza – were located on the Mediterranean coast where their names have been preserved. Ekron and Gath were situated further inland and their location is less certain (see Map 1 and Gazetteer). We have already been informed that a remnant of the Anakim survived in Gaza, Gath, and Ashdod (11 : 22). The Geshurites who also inhabited the coastal area to the south-west are mentioned again in 1 Sam. 27: 8, where we are told that David and his men 'would sally out and raid the Geshurites, the Gizrites, and the Amalekites, for it was they who inhabited the country from Telaim [from of old (?)] all the way to Shur and Egypt'. The relationship between these Geshurites and those of Transjordan is unclear (see 12: 5 and 13: 1–3).

3. Secondary glosses make the syntax of this verse problematic. Its purpose seems to be to specify the territory occupied by the Philistines and Geshurites – i.e. from Ekron to Shihor. Yet, while it is said that this area was ruled by the five lords of the Philistines, we are told as well that it was *reckoned as Canaanite territory*. Finally, at the end of the verse (according to the versification of the Septuagint), reference is made to the Avvites without any indication as to how they fitted into the picture. It reads, literally: 'and the Avvim on the south'. These Avvim are also mentioned in Deut. 2: 23, but no further information is available concerning them.

Shihor appears only four times in the Old Testament (see also 1 Chron. 13: 5; Isa. 23: 3; Jer. 2: 18) and is not spelled consistently in these passages. This is probably the result of attempts to render an Egyptian name into Hebrew – possibly the same name which is rendered 'Shur' in 1 Sam. 27: 8 (see comment on verse 2) and numerous other passages.

4. The term (or name) which defined the southern limits of the Canaanite territory belonging to the Sidonians has been obscured during the process of the transmission of the text. *from the low-lying land* is a conjecture on the part of the translators. Gebal, from which the *Gebalites* derived their name, is identical with Byblos (modern Jebeil). *Aphek* in this passage probably is to be associated with present-day Afqā, approximately 30 kilometres (20 miles) further inland from Jebeil near the sources of Nahr Ibrahim. That being the case, *the Amorite frontier* probably refers to the 'kingdom of Amurru' which is known from other ancient sources to have flourished in the Lebanon area during the fourteenth and thirteenth centuries B.C.

5. *all the Lebanon to the east*: that is, the territory which lay east of the Lebanon Mountain range. *Lebo-hamath*, or 'the entrance of Hamath', marked the northern limits of Israel's ideal territorial claims (see also 2 Kings 14: 25 and Amos 6: 14). Yet the editor has already informed us that Joshua's conquests extended only as far north as Baal-gad (see 11: 17; 12: 7). Thus the territory east of the Lebanon which ideally remained to be occupied was that which lay north of Baal-gad as far as Lebo-hamath. The location of Lebo-hamath is disputed among scholars (see Gazetteer). *

REVIEW OF THE TERRITORY EAST OF THE JORDAN
ASSIGNED TO REUBEN, GAD, AND HALF OF MANASSEH

'Distribute this land now to the nine tribes and half 7
the tribe of Manasseh for their patrimony.' For half the 8
tribe of Manasseh and*a* with them the Reubenites and the

[a] For half...Manasseh and: *prob. rdg.; Heb. om.*

Gadites had each taken their patrimony which Moses
gave them east of the Jordan, as Moses the servant of the
9 LORD had ordained. It started from Aroer which is by
the edge of the gorge of the Arnon, and the level land
half-way along the gorge, and included all the tableland
10 from Medeba as far as Dibon; all the cities of Sihon, the
Amorite king who ruled in Heshbon, as far as the
11 Ammonite frontier; and it also included Gilead and the
Geshurite and Maacathite territory, and all Mount
12 Hermon and the whole of Bashan as far as Salcah, all the
kingdom of Og which he ruled from both Ashtaroth
and Edrei in Bashan. He was a survivor of the remnant
of the Rephaim, but Moses put them both to death and
13 occupied their lands. But the Israelites did not drive out
the Geshurites and the Maacathites; the Geshurites and
14 the Maacathites live among the Israelites to this day. The
tribe of Levi, however, received no patrimony;[a] the
LORD the God of Israel is their patrimony, as he promised
them.

✲ Israel's holdings east of the Jordan which have already
been assigned to Reuben, Gad, and the half tribe of Manasseh
are reviewed again (see 12: 1–6). The summary is followed
by a description of their individual allotments.

9. *and the level land half-way along the gorge*: literally, 'and
the city which is in the middle of the gorge' (see comment on
12: 2). *all the tableland from Medeba as far as Dibon*: the
memorial inscription erected by King Mesha of Moab during
the ninth century B.C. seems to distinguish between the district of Dibon and 'the land of Medeba'. Verse 9 reads literally
'all the tableland of Medeba'; and verse 16 would make more
sense geographically if emended to read 'and included all the

[a] *So Sept.; Heb. adds* the food-offerings of...

tableland *of* Medeba, Heshbon, and all the cities of the table-land'. *Dibon* has been partially excavated by archaeologists (1950–2) and found to have been a flourishing city about 850 B.C. (during the Iron II Age) when it served as Mesha's capital.

13. According to 12: 5 (see comment) the Geshurites and Maacathites had also remained as an independent enclave on the edge of Og's kingdom.

14. *The tribe of Levi, however, received no patrimony*: that is, they received no block of territory. They were assigned cities and surrounding pasture-lands within the territories of the other tribes (see ch. 21). ✳

REUBEN'S ALLOTMENT

So Moses allotted territory to the tribe of the Reuben- 15
ites family by family. Their territory started from Aroer 16
which is by the edge of the gorge of the Arnon, and the
level land half-way along the gorge, and included all the
tableland as far as Medeba; Heshbon and all its cities on 17
the tableland, Dibon, Bamoth-baal, Beth-baal-meon,
Jahaz, Kedemoth, Mephaath, Kiriathaim, Sibmah, Zereth- 18, 1
shahar on the hill in the Vale, Beth-peor, the watershed 20
of Pisgah, and Beth-jeshimoth, all the cities of the table- 21
land, all the kingdom of Sihon the Amorite king who
ruled in Heshbon, whom Moses put to death together
with the princes of Midian, Evi, Rekem, Zur, Hur, and
Reba, the vassals of Sihon who dwelt in the country.
Balaam son of Beor, who practised augury, was among 22
those whom the Israelites put to the sword. The boundary 23
of the Reubenites was the Jordan and the adjacent land:
this is the patrimony of the Reubenites family by family,
both the cities and their hamlets.

✻ The Reubenites received the tableland north of the Arnon, extending as far as Medeba and Heshbon (see comment on 13: 9) and their surrounding cities and villages. The ideal and artificial character of the Deuteronomistic editor's description of the tribal allotments is especially obvious in the case of Reuben. In the oracles of Isa. 15-16 and Jer. 48, most of the territory which was supposedly assigned to this tribe is assumed to be Moabite country. This is confirmed, moreover, by the Mesha inscription which, although it refers to the men of Gad, makes no mention at all of the Reubenites.

18-20. The cities listed here which can be located are not associated specifically with either Medeba or Heshbon; they were scattered throughout the *tableland*.

20. *Beth-peor* deserves special mention. It was from the top of Peor, according to Num. 23: 28, that Baalam issued his third discourse concerning Israel. The Israelites 'joined in the worship of the Baal of Peor' (Num. 25: 3). And Deut. 34: 6 records that Moses 'was buried in a valley in Moab opposite Beth-peor, but to this day no one knows his burial-place'.

21-2. *together with the princes of Midian*: the accounts of Israel's defeat of Sihon in Num. 21: 21-31 and of Baalam's discourses in Num. 22: 2 – 24: 25 represent a different strand of tradition from Num. 25: 6-16 and 31: 1-12 which describe Israel's apostasy at Peor. According to the latter, the apostasy was instigated by the Midianites, especially Baalam the son of 'Beor'; it resulted in a plague; and Israel took vengeance after the plague by executing five Midianite kings. These two strands of traditions have been conflated in the verses under discussion. The five Midianite kings have been reduced to princes and identified as *vassals of Sihon*. And Baalam, who is presented in a rather positive light in Num. 22: 2ff., is represented here as a devious practitioner of *augury*, foretelling the future by interpreting signs and omens. ✻

GAD'S ALLOTMENT

Moses allotted[a] territory to the Gadites family by 24
family. Their territory was Jazer, all the cities of Gilead 25
and half the Ammonite country as far as Aroer which is
east of Rabbah. It reached from Heshbon as far as 26
Ramoth-mizpeh and Betonim, and from Mahanaim as
far as the boundary of Lo-debar; it included in the valley 27
Beth-haram, Beth-nimrah, Succoth, and Zaphon, the
rest of the kingdom of Sihon king of Heshbon. The
boundary was the Jordan and the adjacent land as far as
the end of the Sea of Kinnereth east of the Jordan. This 28
is the patrimony of the Gadites family by family, both
the cities and their hamlets.

✶ Gad received the highlands north of Heshbon (i.e. most of
Gilead and a portion of the Ammonite country) and the strip
of the Arabah which lay east of the Jordan.

25. The location of *Jazer* is uncertain, but it must have been
situated in the highlands north of Heshbon. The Septuagint
version of Num. 21: 24 implies that it was near the Ammonite
frontier. *Aroer*, on the other hand, was situated well within
Ammonite territory. Literally, the text reads: 'as far as Aroer
which is before Rabbah'. *Rabbah* was the chief city of the
Ammonites, and the qualification 'which is before Rabbah'
distinguishes this Aroer (also mentioned in Judg. 11: 33) from
the one which was located further south 'by the edge of the
gorge of the Arnon' (12: 2; 13: 9, 16; etc.). The point of the
verse, then, is that the Gadites occupied Gilead and the vicinity
of Jazer, and even spilled over into Ammonite territory as far
as Aroer, an Ammonite village which must have been situated
slightly to the *west* of Rabbah.

26. The northern limits of Gad's allotment remain obscure,

[a] *So Sept.; Heb. adds* to the tribe of Gad.

since only one of the cities mentioned in this verse can be located with any degree of certainty: *Betonim* can be identified with Khirbet Baṭneh, located about 6 kilometres (4 miles) south-west of Salṭ. It is uncertain whether *Ramoth-mizpeh* is identical with the Mizpah of the Jephthah episode (Judg. 10: 17ff.). A slight emendation is required for the reading *Lo-debar*, which seems justified on the basis of other references in the Old Testament to a city in Transjordan by that name (2 Sam. 9: 4–5; 17: 27; possibly Amos 6: 13). *Mahanaim* served briefly as Ishbosheth's capital (2 Sam. 2: 8ff.); David escaped there during Absalom's rebellion (2 Sam. 17: 24ff.); and one of Solomon's administrative officers resided there (1 Kings 4: 14).

27. *in the valley*: that is, in the Arabah east of the Jordan. *Succoth* was partially excavated by archaeologists between 1960 and 1964. The city seems to have flourished during the Late Bronze Age, at which time it boasted an impressive sanctuary. It was destroyed soon thereafter and apparently reoccupied by a semi-nomadic group. The probable site of *Zaphon* has also been excavated in recent years (1964–7; see Gazetteer), but its location is less certain. ✳

THE HALF TRIBE OF MANASSEH'S ALLOTMENT

29 Moses allotted territory to the half tribe of Manasseh: it was for half the tribe of the Manassites family by family.
30 Their territory ran from Mahanaim and included all Bashan, all the kingdom of Og king of Bashan and all
31 Havvoth-jair in Bashan – sixty cities. Half Gilead, and Ashtaroth and Edrei the royal cities of Og in Bashan, belong to the sons of Machir son of Manasseh on behalf of half the Machirites family by family.
32 These are the territories which Moses allotted to the tribes as their patrimonies in the lowlands of Moab east

of the Jordan.[a] But to the tribe of Levi he gave no 33
patrimony: the LORD the God of Israel is their patrimony,
as he promised them.

✶ The half tribe of Manasseh received Bashan and a portion
of Gilead (as far as Mahanaim; see verse 26) as its allotment.
Verses 32-3 conclude the description of the allotments east
of the Jordan and remind the reader again (see 13: 14) that
the Levites received a different kind of inheritance from the
other tribes.

30. *and all Havvoth-jair in Bashan*: the geographical relationship between Argob, *Bashan*, and *Havvoth-jair* is unclear.
Deut. 3: 13-14, which has obviously influenced this
verse, quotes Moses as saying: 'The rest of Gilead and the
whole of Bashan the kingdom of Og, all the region of Argob,
I assigned to half the tribe of Manasseh. (...Jair son of
Manasseh took all the region of Argob as far as the Geshurite
and Maacathite border. There are tent-villages in Bashan still
called by his name, Havvoth-jair.)' Judg. 10: 3, on the other
hand, identifies the Jair after whom Havvoth-jair was named
as a Gileadite who judged Israel for twenty-two years.
Havvoth means 'encampments' or 'tent-villages'.

31. The text should be emended (with Codex Alexandrinus,
a fourth-century manuscript of the Septuagint) to read: 'on
behalf of the Manassites family by family'. This verse suggests
– and it will become even more obvious in the treatment of
Manasseh west of the Jordan (see especially 17: 1-6) – that
the concept of the half tribe of Manasseh east of the Jordan is
an artificial one. Specifically, it was not Manasseh but the
Machirites who settled in Gilead and Bashan. ✶

TERRITORIAL ALLOTMENTS TO JUDAH AND JOSEPH

Now follow the possessions which the Israelites **14**
acquired in the land of Canaan, as Eleazar the priest,

[a] So Pesh.; Heb. adds Jericho.

Joshua son of Nun, and the heads of the families of the
2 Israelite tribes allotted them. They were assigned by lot,
following the LORD's command given through Moses, to
3 the nine and a half tribes. To two and a half tribes Moses
had given patrimonies beyond the Jordan; but he gave
4 none to the Levites as he did to the others. The tribe of
Joseph formed the two tribes of Manasseh and Ephraim.
The Levites were given no share in the land, only cities
to dwell in, with their common land for flocks and herds.
5 So the Israelites, following the LORD's command given to
Moses, assigned the land.

* Having reviewed now the first phase of the tribal allotments – i.e. the assignments made by Moses to Reuben, Gad,
and the half tribe of Manasseh while Israel was still camped
in Transjordan – the editor begins his account of the second
phase, i.e. the distribution of territory to the houses of Judah
and Joseph. Joshua is aided by Eleazar the priest, and the scene
of the distribution seems to be the camp at Gilgal (cp. 4: 19;
5: 10; 9: 6; 14: 6). The third and final phase of the distribution
will occur at Shiloh where Joshua is aided by a representative
group of leaders from the various tribes (18: 1–10). The
Deuteronomistic editor does not specifically indicate why the
houses of Judah and Joseph should have been given preferen-
tial treatment; although he may have intended a contrast
between the aggressiveness of these two houses (see 14: 6ff.;
17: 14ff.) and the failure of the remaining tribes to appropriate
territory even after it 'lay subdued at their feet' (18: 1–3).

1. *Eleazar the priest*, who assists Joshua in the allotment of
territory to the tribes, is identified throughout the later strata
of the Old Testament as the son of Aaron (e.g. Exod. 6: 25;
Lev. 10: 5; Num. 3: 2). Obviously there is some connection
between these Eleazar traditions, however, and the older ones
concerning Eli, a local priest at Shiloh (1 Sam. 1–6). Note, for

example, that both Eleazar and Eli have sons named Phinehas (Josh. 22: 13, 30–2; 24: 33; 1 Sam. 1: 3; 2: 34). 'Eli' is an abbreviated form of 'Eleazar' and it may be that, due to this similarity in names, elements of tradition originally associated with one of these figures have been transferred to the other.

2. The use of the *lot* is reported numerous times in the Old Testament (e.g. 7: 10–16), but the contexts do not enable us to establish the character and form of the lot in ancient Israel.

3–4. Theoretically, Israel was composed of twelve tribes, each descended from one of the sons of Jacob. It becomes apparent from a close reading of the earlier strata of the Old Testament, however, that this genealogy is an over-simplification. The Deuteronomistic editor encountered redactional problems in this regard, since the traditions which he incorporated into his account of the tribal allotments did not always recognize the same tribal divisions or even necessarily presuppose the twelve-tribe scheme. At least one of these traditions, for example, treated the 'tribe (or house) of Joseph' as a single unit and assumed that Joseph received a single lot (see 17: 14–18). Other traditions which he included made a sharp distinction between the two major Josephite tribes, Ephraim and Manasseh (see 16: 5–8; 17: 7–10). Thus, lest any confusion should arise, the editor explains in advance that *the tribe of Joseph formed the two tribes of Manasseh and Ephraim*. We have already seen that he incorporated the Machirites into the twelve-tribe scheme by treating them as Manassites (see comment on 13: 31). The Calebites will be included under Judah in a similar fashion (14: 6–15; 15: 13–19). *

THE CALEBITES RECEIVE A SPECIAL ALLOTMENT

Now the tribe of Judah had come to Joshua in Gilgal, 6 and Caleb son of Jephunneh the Kenizzite said to him, 'You remember what the LORD said to Moses the man of God concerning you and me at Kadesh-barnea. I was 7 forty years old when Moses the servant of the LORD sent me from there to explore the land, and I brought back 8 an honest report. The others who went with me discouraged the people, but I loyally carried out the purpose 9 of the LORD my God. Moses swore an oath that day and said, "The land on which you have set foot shall be your patrimony and your sons' after you as a possession for ever; for you have loyally carried out the purpose of the 10 LORD my God." Well, the LORD has spared my life as he promised; it is now forty-five years since he made this promise to Moses, at the time when Israel was journeying 11 in the wilderness. Today I am eighty-five years old. I am still as strong as I was on the day when Moses sent me out; I am as fit now for war as I was then and am ready to take 12 the field again. Give me today this hill-country which the LORD then promised me. You heard on that day that the Anakim were there and their cities were large and well fortified. Perhaps the LORD will be with me and I shall 13 dispossess them as he promised.' Joshua blessed Caleb and 14 gave him Hebron for his patrimony, and that is why Hebron remains to this day in the patrimony of Caleb son of Jephunneh the Kenizzite. It is because he loyally carried out the purpose of the LORD the God of Israel. 15 Formerly the name of Hebron was Kiriath-arba. This Arba was the chief man of the Anakim. And the land was at peace.

* The Calebites received Hebron as a special allotment as a reward for the courage and religious zeal which Caleb had demonstrated when he served among the spies whom Moses sent to reconnoitre the land of Canaan. Both this passage and another concerning Caleb (15: 13–19) disrupt the otherwise carefully organized presentation of the tribal allotments. It has been argued, therefore, that both have been inserted secondarily: 14: 6–15 originally followed 11: 21–3 and 15: 13–19 depends upon Judg. 1: 10–20.

6. *Caleb son of Jephunneh the Kenizzite*: Caleb is identified as a Judahite in several Old Testament passages (e.g. Num. 13: 6; 34: 19), but as a Kenizzite in others (e.g. Num. 32: 12). The Kenizzites apparently were an Edomite tribal group (Gen. 36: 11, 15, 42) which settled in the southern hill-country and was eventually assimilated into Judah.

7–9. Num. 13–14 (see also Deut. 1: 20–45) describes how Caleb had distinguished himself as a man of courage and religious zeal. The spies whom Moses sent to reconnoitre the promised land returned with glowing reports about its fertility, but with equally terrifying warnings concerning the strength of its cities and the gigantic stature of the men who inhabited them. All except Caleb and Joshua advised against invasion. They alone contended that Israel's God could and would lead her to victory. When the assembly chose to heed the warning of the majority of the spies, God decreed that the conquest be delayed until that whole generation, save Caleb and Joshua alone, had died. The promise that Caleb would be given the land on which he had set foot is not indicated in the account of Num. 13–14, but it is presupposed in Deut. 1: 36.

12. According to 11: 21–2, Joshua had already conquered the hill-country and cleared the *Anakim* from it. But this verse seems to assume that they still remained there in possession. Note that the parallel passage in Judg. 1: 8–10 attributes the conquest of the southern hill-country to 'the men of Judah'.

14–15. According to Num. 13: 22, *Hebron* was built seven years before Zoan (possibly Avaris) of Egypt. The city was to play an important role in Israel's history, serving, for example, as the first capital of David's kingdom. The biblical writers equate it with both Mamre, where Abraham sojourned (Gen. 13: 18; 23: 19), and Kiriath-arba, where Sarah died (Gen.

23: 2; 35: 27). Excavations at Hebron indicate intermittent occupation from as early as the Middle Bronze Age.

The name *Kiriath-arba* is explained in this passage as meaning 'the village of Arba', Arba being 'the chief man of the Anakim' (see also 15: 13 and 21: 12). But *Arba* means 'four' in Hebrew and probably would not have been used as a proper noun. Actually, the Septuagint provides a preferable reading: 'The name of Hebron was originally Kiriath-arba, the *metropolis* of the Anakim.' *

JUDAH'S ALLOTMENT: HER BOUNDARIES

15 This is the territory allotted to the tribe of the sons of Judah family by family. It started from the Edomite frontier at the wilderness of Zin and ran as far as the
2 Negeb at its southern end, and it had a common border with the Negeb at the end of the Dead Sea, where an
3 inlet of water bends towards the Negeb. It continued from the south by the ascent of Akrabbim, passed by Zin, went up from the south of Kasesh-barnea, passed by
4 Hezron, went on to Addar and turned round to Karka. It then passed along to Azmon, reached the Torrent of Egypt, and its limit was the sea. This was their[a] southern boundary.

5 The eastern boundary is the Dead Sea as far as the mouth of the Jordan and the adjacent land northwards from the
6 inlet of the sea, at the mouth of the Jordan. The boundary goes up to Beth-hoglah; it passes north of Beth-arabah
7 and thence to the stone of Bohan son of Reuben, thence to Debir from the Vale of Achor, and then turns north to the districts[b] in front of the ascent of Adummim south of the gorge. The boundary then passes the waters of

[a] So Sept.; Heb. your.   [b] Prob. rdg., cp. 18: 17; Heb. to Gilgal.

En-shemesh and the limit there is En-rogel. It then goes 8
up by the Valley of Ben-hinnom to the southern slope
of the Jebusites (that is Jerusalem). Thence it goes up to
the top of the hill which faces the Valley of Hinnom on
the west; this is at the northern end of the Vale of Rephaim. The boundary then bends round from the top of 9
the hill to the spring of the waters of Nephtoah, runs
round to the cities of Mount Ephron and round to Baalah,
that is Kiriath-jearim. It then continues westwards from 10
Baalah to Mount Seir, passes on to the north side of the
slope of Mount Jearim, that is Kesalon, down to Beth-
shemesh and on to Timnah. The boundary then goes 11
north to the slope of Ekron, bends round to Shikkeron,
crosses to Mount Baalah and reaches Jabneel; its limit is
the sea. The western boundary is the Great Sea and the 12
land adjacent. This is the whole circuit of the boundary
of the tribe of Judah family by family.

✵ The whole of ch. 15 is concerned with Judah's territorial
allotment, but four divisions are easily discernible within it:
verses 1–12 describe Judah's boundaries; verses 13–19 provide
further traditions concerning the Calebites who are treated
as a sub-grouping of Judah (see 14: 6); an extensive list of
Judahite cities is recorded in verses 20–62; and verse 63 explains
why Jerusalem does not appear in the city list. The Calebite
paragraph disrupts the description of the territorial allotment
somewhat and is an almost word-for-word duplicate of Judg.
1: 10–15. It may have been derived from the latter passage by
a post-Deuteronomistic editor or scribe and inserted here with
slight modifications (see comment on 14: 6–15). The other
three divisions of ch. 15, on the other hand, are derived from
mutually independent traditions, quite possibly written
sources, to which the Deuteronomistic editor had access.

The description of Judah's boundary is based on a list of crucial boundary points (mostly cities) which also involved several of the other tribes. The editor seems to have been relying on this same boundary tradition, for example, in his description of the territorial allotments to Ephraim (16: 2–3, 5–8), Manasseh (17: 7–10), Benjamin (18: 12–19), Zebulun (19: 10–16), Issachar (19: 17–23), Asher (19: 24–31), Naphtali (19: 32–9), and Dan (19: 40–8). Whether the boundary list provided specific information concerning the Transjordanian tribes is uncertain. It apparently did not for Simeon.

1–4. This description of Judah's southern boundary corresponds almost word-for-word to the southern frontier of the land of Canaan as described in Num. 34: 3–5. The fact that verse 1 (paralleled by Num. 34: 3) presupposes an *Edomite frontier* west of the Arabah is significant. Edom does seem to have expanded her authority in that direction, but probably not until the last years of the Judaean kingdom. The reference could possibly be to the Amalekite inhabitants of Sinai and the southern Negeb (see especially 1 Sam. 15: 7) who were recognized as an Edomite tribe (Gen. 36: 12; 1 Chron. 1: 36).

6–11. Judah's northern boundary, which is traced in considerable detail from east to west, corresponds to the southern boundaries of Benjamin and Dan. Thus much of the same boundary will be described again in connection with Benjamin's allotment (18: 14–19), and several of the border cities mentioned again in connection with Dan (19: 40–8). The eastern and western segments of this common boundary can be traced fairly easily (see Map 4). But none of the boundary points between *the ascent of Adummim* (present-day Ṭalʿat ed-Damm) and *the waters of Nephtoah* (present-day Me Neftoah) can be located with certainty. It is implied in 2 Sam. 17: 17 and 1 Kings 1: 9, 41 that *En-rogel* – which means 'spring of the traveller' or 'spring of the spy' – was within hearing distance, yet out of sight of *Jerusalem*. ʿAin Madowerah, north-east of Jerusalem near ʿIsawiyeh, would meet both of these qualifications. Jer. 19 seems at first glance to place *the Valley of Ben-hinnom* immediately outside the gates of Jerusalem (see especially verse 2), but this evidence disappears when the composite nature of the chapter is taken into account. Verse 8 of the boundary description includes a notation which actually equates *the Jebusites* (literally, 'the Jebusite') with *Jerusalem*. But this is clearly a secondary scribal note (see also 18: 28 and Judg. 19: 10), and its validity is open to question on at least three grounds: (1) That 'the Jebusite' was an earlier name for Jerusalem would have been a tempting scribal inference, especially in the light of 2 Sam. 5: 6–8. Compare, for example, the Chronicler's restatement of the latter passage in 1 Chron. 11: 4–6. (2) The equation of 'the Jebusite' with Jerusalem implies that the Judah–Benjamin boundary made a radical dip to the south at Jerusalem, a dip which is unexplainable on geographical grounds. One would rather have expected the boundary to follow a more direct route between the ascent of Adummim and the waters of Nephtoah, where a series of valleys would have provided a more natural division. (3) Since the boundary is said to have crossed *the southern slope* of 'the Jebusite', the result of the Jebusite/Jerusalem equation is to place Jerusalem on the Benjamite side. This too is difficult to explain with regard to Israel's early tribal history. We can be certain in any case that the boundary crossed the central hill-country fairly near to Jerusalem. But the possibility must be considered in the light of these three factors that 'the Jebusite', rather than being identical with Jerusalem, was actually situated slightly further to the north. This would mean that the boundary also passed to the north. The Jebusite/Jerusalem problem will arise again in connection with 15: 63 and 18: 28.

Secondary notations also equate *Baalah*, Kiriath-baal (see verse 60) and *Kiriath-jearim*, while implying a distinction between these three and *Mount Jearim* (see also 18: 14–16). Possibly Baalah was a sanctuary near Kiriath-jearim in accordance with which the latter could also be called Kiriath-

baal(ah) – i.e. 'the village of Baal(ah)'. Mount Jearim was
probably the mountain on which Kiriath-jearim was situated,
however, and can hardly have been identical with *Kesalon*.

12. *The western boundary is the Great Sea*: thus Judah's
allotment theoretically included the Philistine and Geshurite
territory which remained to be occupied (cp. 13: 1–3). *

THE CONQUESTS OF CALEB AND OTHNIEL

13 Caleb son of Jephunneh received his share of the land
within the tribe of Judah as the LORD had said to Joshua.
It was Kiriath-arba, that is Hebron. This Arba was the
14 ancestor of the Anakim. Caleb drove out the three
Anakim: these were Sheshai, Ahiman and Talmai, descen-
15 dants of Anak. From there he attacked the inhabitants of
Debir; the name of Debir was formerly Kiriath-sepher.
16 Caleb announced that whoever should attack Kiriath-
sepher and capture it would receive his daughter Achsah
17 in marriage. Othniel, son of Caleb's brother Kenaz, cap-
18 tured it, and Caleb gave him his daughter Achsah. When
she came to him, he incited her*[a]* to ask her father for
a piece of land. As she sat on the ass, she made a noise, and
19 Caleb asked her, 'What did you mean by that?' She
replied, 'I want a favour from you. You have put me in
this dry Negeb; you must give me pools of water as well.'
So Caleb gave her the upper pool and the lower pool.

* Caleb drives out the three Anakim from Hebron; Othniel
captures Debir at Caleb's instigation; Achsah, Caleb's daughter, is given in marriage to Othniel as a reward for his deed;
and Caleb, upon her request, gives Othniel two pools of water.
As noted above, this paragraph parallels Judg. 1: 10–15 and

[a] *So some Sept. MSS.; Heb.* she incited him.

may have been inserted into the description of Judah's territorial allotment by a post-Deuteronomistic redactor or scribe.

14. The parallel passage in Judg. 1: 8ff. attributes the conquest of Hebron to the men of Judah in general. Num. 13: 22 states that the three descendents of Anak, *Sheshai*, *Ahiman* and *Talmai*, were already living at Hebron when Moses sent spies to survey the promised land. Here again the Septuagint reads, 'Kiriath-arba the metropolis of the Anakim' (see comment on 14: 14–15).

15. The precise location of *Debir* is uncertain, although it was obviously situated in the hill-country not far from Hebron (see also 10: 38–9; 11: 21). Note that, while it is equated with *Kiriath-sepher* in this passage, it is equated with Kiriath-sannah in the city list (15: 49).

17. We are told in another context that Othniel defeated Cushan-rishathaim king of Aram and judged Israel for forty years thereafter (Judg. 3: 7–11).

18. The context clearly supports the N.E.B. translation of the Septuagint, *he incited her*, rather than the Hebrew, 'she incited him'. The N.E.B. translation *she made a noise* is somewhat less convincing, however, the meaning of the crucial verb having been lost through the ages. The problematic verb appears only here, in the parallel passage (Judg. 1: 14), and in Judg. 4: 21 (translated 'oozed out' in the N.E.B.). The R.S.V. translators rendered it 'and she alighted from her ass'. In any case, the original purpose of this notation probably was to explain why the Othnielites of Debir had access to pools of water which might otherwise be expected to belong to the inhabitants of Hebron. ✳

JUDAH'S ALLOTMENT: HER CITIES

This is the patrimony of the tribe of the sons of Judah 20 family by family. These are the cities belonging to the 21 tribe of Judah, the full count. By the Edomite frontier

22 in the Negeb: Kabzeel, Eder, Jagur, Kinah, Dimonah,
23, 24 Ararah,*a* Kedesh, Hazor,*b* Ithnan, Ziph,*b* Telem, Bealoth,
25, 26 Hazor-hadattah,*b* Kerioth-hezron,*c* Amam, Shema, Mola-
27, 28 dah, Hazar-gaddah, Heshmon,*b* Beth-pelet, Hazar-shual,
29, 30 Beersheba and its villages,*d* Baalah, Iyim,*e* Ezem, Eltolad,
31, 32 Kesil, Hormah, Ziklag, Madmannah, Sansannah, Lebaoth, Shilhim, Ain, and Rimmon: in all, twenty-nine cities with their hamlets.

33, 34 In the Shephelah: Eshtaol, Zorah, Ashnah, Zanoah,
35 En-gannim, Tappuah, Enam, Jarmuth, Adullam, Socoh,
36 Azekah, Shaaraim, Adithaim, Gederah, namely both parts
37 of Gederah: fourteen cities with their hamlets. Zenan,
38, 39 Hadashah, Migdal-gad, Dilan, Mizpeh, Joktheel, Lachish,
40, 41 Bozkath, Eglon, Cabbon, Lahmas,*f* Kithlish, Gederoth, Beth-dagon, Naamah, and Makkedah: sixteen cities with
42, 43 their hamlets. Libnah, Ether,*g* Ashan, Jiphtah, Ashnah,
44 Nezib, Keilah, Achzib, and Mareshah: nine cities with
45, 46 their hamlets. Ekron, with its villages and hamlets, and from Ekron westwards, all the cities near Ashdod and
47 their hamlets. Ashdod with its villages and hamlets, Gaza with its villages and hamlets as far as the Torrent of Egypt and the Great Sea and the land adjacent.

48, 49 In the hill-country: Shamir, Jattir, Socoh, Dannah,
50 Kiriath-sannah, that is Debir, Anab, Eshtemoh, Anim,
51 Goshen, Holon, and Giloh: eleven cities in all with their
52, 53 hamlets. Arab, Dumah, Eshan, Janim, Beth-tappuah,

[*a*] *Prob. rdg.; Heb.* Adadah.   [*b*] *Omitted by Sept.*
[*c*] *So Pesh.; Heb. adds* that is Hazor.
[*d*] its villages: *so Sept.; Heb.* Biziothiah.
[*e*] *Omitted in 19: 3 (cp. 1 Chr. 4: 29).*
[*f*] *Or, with some MSS.,* Lahman.
[*g*] *Or, with 1 Sam. 30: 30,* Athak.

Aphek,[a] Humtah, Kiriath-arba, that is Hebron, and Zior: 54
nine cities in all with their hamlets. Maon, Carmel, Ziph, 55
Juttah, Jezreel, Jokdeam, Zanoah, Cain, Gibeah, and 56,57
Timnah: ten cities in all with their hamlets. Halhul, 58
Beth-zur, Gedor, Maarath, Beth-anoth, and Eltekon: 59
six cities in all with their hamlets. Tekoa, Ephrathah,
that is Bethlehem, Peor, Etam, Culom, Tatam, Sores,
Carem, Gallim, Baither, and Manach: eleven cities in all
with their hamlets.[b] Kiriath-baal, that is Kiriath-jearim, 60
and Rabbah: two cities with their hamlets.

In the wilderness: Beth-arabah, Middin, Secacah, Nib- 61,62
shan, Ir-melach, and En-gedi: six cities with their hamlets.

At Jerusalem, the men of Judah were unable to drive 63
out the Jebusites who lived there, and to this day Jebusites
and men of Judah live together in Jerusalem.

* The cities assigned to Judah are listed in geographically
coherent groupings, each list concluding with a sub-total.
The cities assigned to Benjamin (18: 21-8) are treated similarly; the editor apparently derived both lists from the same
source. When the Judahite and Benjamite lists are combined,
twelve sub-groupings of cities emerge which most scholars
believe correspond to the twelve administrative districts of
the kingdom of Judah. These are:

I. The Negeb district (15: 21–32)
II–IV. The three Shephelah districts (15: 33–6, 37-41, 42–3)
V–XI. The seven hill-country districts (15: 48–51, 52–4,
  55-7, 58-9; the Septuagint addition to 59; 15:60 with 18:
  25-8; 18: 21-4)
XII. The wilderness district (15: 61–2)

Map 3 includes only those cities which can be located with
some degree of certainty.

[a] *Or* Aphekah.   [b] Tekoa...hamlets: *so Sept.; Heb. om.*

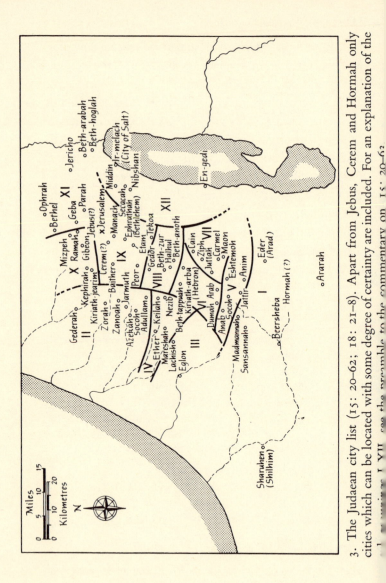

3. The Judaean city list (15: 20–62; 18: 21–8). Apart from Jebus, Cerem and Hormah only cities which can be located with some degree of certainty are included. For an explanation of the numerals I–XII, see the preamble to the commentary on 15: 20–62.

21–32. *in the Negeb*: *Eder* should be emended with the Septuagint to read 'Arad'. The site has been excavated in recent years and found to have been a flourishing city during the Early Bronze Age. The kings of Judah later maintained a fortress there for the protection of Judah's southern frontier. *Beersheba*, which is being excavated currently (1973), was also a fortress city during the period of the divided kingdoms. Thus far no evidence has been uncovered which indicates the existence of a city at the site before the Iron Age. *Shilhim* is to be equated with Sharuhen (cp. 19: 6).

33–43. *In the Shephelah*: only two of the cities in the third Shephelah district can be identified with any degree of certainty: *Lachish* and *Eglon*, both of which have been extensively excavated by archaeologists.

44–7. The list has been expanded secondarily at this point in order to include the Philistine territory. See verse 12.

48–60. *In the hill-country*: five of the seven hill-country districts and a portion of another (verse 60) are introduced in connection with Judah's allotment. These are listed in geographical order from south to north. The remainder of the hill-country cities have been detached from the list and incorporated into the description of Benjamin's allotment (see comment on 18: 21–8). Note that *Kiriath-sannah* is identified here as *Debir*, in contrast to 15: 15 which equated Debir with Kiriath-sepher. *Gallim*, which appears in verse 59 (supplied on the basis of the Septuagint), cannot be located precisely. But Isa. 10: 30 clearly places it to the north-east of Jerusalem. This implies, of course, that the ninth district also extended further north than Jerusalem and renders problematic the notations in Josh. 15: 8 and 18: 28 which equate Jerusalem with Jebus of the tenth district (cp. comments on 15: 8, 18: 25–8; and 'Jebus' in the Gazetteer).

61–2. *In the wilderness*: *Ir-melach*, 'the city of salt', is probably to be identified with Khirbet Qumran, where the so-called 'Dead Sea Scrolls' were discovered and where Iron Age remains have been unearthed beneath the debris of the

Hellenistic and Roman periods. See 'Middin' in the Gazetteer for the probable location of *Middin, Secacah,* and *Nibshan.* The name *En-gedi* is still preserved in that of 'En-Gedi; situated on the western bank of the Dead Sea.

63. Judg. 1: 21, 27–34 (35–6?) provides a list of un-conquered cities which lay within the territories of certain of the tribes. Much of this list has been incorporated in frag-mentary fashion into the book of Joshua (compare this verse and 16: 10; 17: 11–13 and 19: 29*b*–30). There are, of course, some differences in the two versions of the list, but these differences seem to be due in most cases to post-Deuterono-mistic editing. Verse 63 (paralleled by Judg. 1: 21) is an example. The two verses correspond almost word for word, except that the Joshua version attributes the failure to drive out the *Jebusites* from Jerusalem to *the men of Judah,* while the Judges version attributes it to 'the Benjamites'. The question arises again, therefore, whether 'the Jebusite' has been cor-rectly identified with Jerusalem and, accordingly, whether Jerusalem was situated on the Judahite or the Benjamite side of the tribal boundary (see comment on 15: 6–11 and 'Jebus' in the Gazetteer). Judg. 1: 21, at least in its present form, presupposes the identity of the two and that Jerusalem lay within Benjamite territory. This verse presupposes neither, in spite of the fact that one of the notations which equates 'the Jebusite' with Jerusalem appears earlier in the same chapter (verse 8). ✳

JOSEPH'S ALLOTMENT: EPHRAIM

16 This is the lot that fell to the sons of Joseph: the boun-dary runs from the Jordan at Jericho, east of the waters of Jericho by the wilderness, and goes up from Jericho
2 into the hill-country to Bethel. It runs on from Bethel to
3 Luz and crosses the Archite border at Ataroth.[a] West-wards it descends to the boundary of the Japhletites as far

[a] Ataroth-addar *in 16: 5; 18: 13.*

as the boundary of Lower Beth-horon and Gezer; its
limit is the sea. Here Manasseh and Ephraim the sons of 4
Joseph received their patrimony.

This was the boundary of the Ephraimites family by 5
family: their eastern boundary ran from Ataroth-addar
up to Upper Beth-horon. It continued westwards to 6
Michmethath on the north, going round by the east of
Taanath-shiloh and passing by it on the east of Janoah.
It descends from Janoah to Ataroth and Naarath, touches 7
Jericho and continues to the Jordan, and from Tappuah 8
it goes westwards by the gorge of Kanah; and its limit is
the sea. This is the patrimony of the tribe of Ephraim
family by family. There were also cities reserved for 9
the Ephraimites within the patrimony of the Manassites,
each of these cities with its hamlets. They did not however 10
drive out the Canaanites who dwelt in Gezer; the
Canaanites have lived among the Ephraimites to the
present day but have been subject to forced labour in
perpetuity.

✻ Chs. 16 and 17 describe the allotment to the sons of Joseph,
who are subdivided into the Ephraimites (16: 5–10) and the
Manassites (17: 1–13). The passage 16: 1–4 introduces this
description by defining Joseph's southern limits. Specifically,
this line is Ephraim's southern boundary, the eastern portion
of which corresponds to Benjamin's northern border (see
18: 12–14 and Map 4). The remainder of ch. 16 completes
the description of Ephraim's territory.

1–4. The southern boundary of Joseph (Ephraim) began at
the Jordan near *Jericho* and passed through the hill-country
near *Bethel* to *Lower Beth-horon*. The location of *Ataroth* (or
Ataroth-addar as it appears in 16: 5 and 18: 13) is problematic
(see Gazetteer). The Archites and *Japhletites* are otherwise

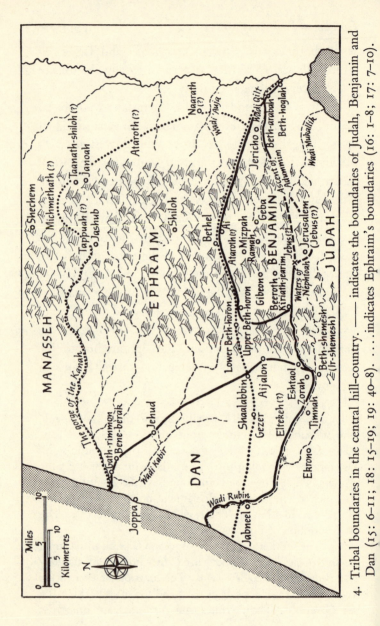

4. Tribal boundaries in the central hill-country. —— indicates the boundaries of Judah, Benjamin and Dan (15: 6–11; 18: 15–19; 19: 40–8). ···· indicates Ephraim's boundaries (16: 1–8; 17: 7–10).

unknown in the Old Testament, except for Hushai the Archite who served as a counsellor to David (2 Sam. 15: 32; 16: 16).

From *Lower Beth-horon* the boundary is said to have crossed to *Gezer* and continued to the Mediterranean Sea. This last segment is inconsistent with the boundary system as other-wise presented, however, in that it cuts across the territory allotted to Dan (see 19: 40–8 and Map 4). Apparently this portion of the boundary description has been revised on the basis of the list of unconquered cities, which specifically associates Gezer with Ephraim (see comments on 15: 63 and verse 10 below).

5–7. These verses have become obscured during the process of transmission and make little geographical sense as they stand now. Verses 5b–6a must be interpreted as an abbreviated summary of Ephraim's southern boundary rather than her eastern limits. Literally, it reads, 'the boundary went out to the sea' rather than *It continued westwards to Michmethath on the north*. 'Michmethath on the north' appears abruptly in the Hebrew text, and only *Janoah* and *Jericho* of the boundary points which follow in verse 7 can be located with any degree of certainty. However, Michmethath, *Taanath-shiloh*, and Janoah all appear to have been located in the vicinity of Shechem (see comments on verses 17: 7–10a below). It is unclear whether the *Ataroth* of verse 7 is identical with the one mentioned in verses 3 and 5. If so, the Ataroth–Naarath–Jericho–Jordan segment of Ephraim's boundary seems mean-ingless. If not, then we may suppose that the intention of verse 7 is to describe Ephraim's eastern boundary and search for Ataroth and Naarath somewhere roughly between Jericho and Janoah (see Map 4 and comments on the individual sites in the Gazetteer).

8. The description makes a new beginning now at *Tappuah*, which cannot be located precisely but lay between Mich-methath and Jashub – i.e. near the sources of the *gorge of Kanah*, south-west of Shechem (see comment on 17: 7–10a). The gorge of Kanah (present-day Wadi Qāna which flows

into the Jarkon) apparently served as the boundary between Ephraim and Manasseh from Tappuah to the Mediterranean Sea.

10. *They did not...drive out the Canaanites who dwelt in Gezer*: here again the editor depends upon the list of unconquered cities which is reproduced in full in Judg. 1: 21, 27–35 (see especially verse 29). Archaeological excavations at Gezer indicate that the city flourished during the Middle and Late Bronze Ages. *

JOSEPH'S ALLOTMENT: MANASSEH

17 This is the territory allotted to the tribe of Manasseh, Joseph's eldest son. Machir was Manasseh's eldest son and father of Gilead, a fighting man; Gilead and Bashan were allotted to him.

2 The rest of the Manassites family by family were the sons of Abiezer, the sons of Helek, the sons of Asriel, the sons of Shechem, the sons of Hepher, and the sons of Shemida; these were the male offspring of Manasseh son of Joseph family by family.

3 Zelophehad son of Hepher, son of Gilead, son of Machir, son of Manasseh, had no sons but only daughters: their names were Mahlah, Noah, Hoglah, Milcah and 4 Tirzah. They presented themselves before Eleazar the priest and Joshua son of Nun, and before the chiefs, and they said, 'The LORD commanded Moses to allow us to inherit on the same footing as our kinsmen.' They were therefore given a patrimony on the same footing as their father's brothers according to the commandment of the LORD.

5 There fell to Manasseh's lot ten shares, apart from the 6 country of Gilead and Bashan beyond the Jordan, because

Manasseh's daughters had received a patrimony on the same footing as his sons. The country of Gilead belonged to the rest of Manasseh's sons. The boundary of Manasseh 7 reached from Asher as far as Michmethath, which is to the east of Shechem, and thence southwards towards Jashub by[a] En-tappuah. The territory of Tappuah be- 8 longed to Manasseh, but Tappuah itself was on the border of Manasseh and belonged to Ephraim. The boundary 9 then followed the gorge of Kanah to the south of the gorge (these cities[b] belong to Ephraim, although they lie among the cities of Manasseh), the boundary of Manasseh being on the north of the gorge; its limit was the sea. The southern side belonged to Ephraim and the 10 northern to Manasseh, and their[c] boundary was the sea. They marched with Asher on the north and Issachar on the east. But in Issachar and Asher, Manasseh possessed 11 Beth-shean and its villages, Ibleam and its villages, the inhabitants of Dor and its villages, the inhabitants of En-dor and its villages, the inhabitants of Taanach and its villages, and the inhabitants of Megiddo and its villages. (The third is the district of Dor.[d]) The Manassites were 12 unable to occupy these cities; the Canaanites maintained their hold on that part of the country. When the Israelites 13 grew stronger, they put the Canaanites to forced labour, but they did not drive them out.

☆ The sub-tribal groupings which composed Manasseh are delineated by means of a genealogical formulation (verses 1–6). Special attention is given to the Machirites in Trans-

[a] Jashub by: *prob. rdg.; Heb.* the inhabitants of.
[b] these cities: *prob. rdg.; Heb. obscure.*   [c] *So Sept.; Heb.* his.
[d] The third...Dor: *prob. rdg.; Heb.* The three districts.

jordan and the families which traced their ancestry to the daughters of Zelophehad. The genealogy is followed by a description of Manasseh's boundaries (verses 7-10) and a curious reference to several cities in Issachar and Asher which Manasseh possessed but was unable to occupy (verses 10-13).

1. *Machir* accounts for the 'half tribe of Manasseh' which, according to 12: 6 and 13: 29-31, had received a territorial allotment east of the Jordan. Note, however, that the Song of Deborah mentions Machir instead of Manasseh in association with certain of the west Jordanian tribes.

> The men of Ephraim showed a brave front in the vale,
> crying, 'With you, Benjamin! Your clansmen are here!'
> From Machir down came the marshals,
> from Zebulun the bearers of the musterer's staff. (Judg.
> 5: 14)

This text has led some scholars to conclude that the Machirites were once settled in the central (Manassite) hill-country west of the Jordan and later migrated across the Jordan to Gilead and Bashan.

2-4. The genealogical tradition presented here closely parallels that of Num. 26: 28-34 yet contrasts with the one presented in 1 Chron. 7: 14-19. Several of the same names appear in the Chronicler's version, but in a different arrangement. It is unclear why some of the Manassite families are identified as descendants of the sons of Manasseh while others are said to have descended from the daughters of Zelophehad. The same distinction is maintained in Num. 26: 33-4; 27: 1-11; and 36: 1-12. The gloss in verse 3 which identifies Zelophehad's father, Hepher, as a *Son of Gilead, son of Machir, son of Manasseh* is missing in the Septuagint and finds no support in the parallel genealogy of Num. 26: 28-34.

5-6. In all, then, Manasseh's lot would have consisted of twelve shares: two (Gilead and Bashan) were given to the Machirites; five to the families descended from the daughters of Zelophehad son of Hepher; and five to the families des-

cended from the remaining sons of Manasseh (i.e. excluding
Machir and Hepher).

7–10*a*. Manasseh's territory touched Asher's allotment in
the north (see 19: 24–31) and was bounded by Ephraim in the
south. The editor has already described the line which Manasseh shared with Ephraim (16: 6–8). Now he describes it again
in somewhat more detail. We learn that *Michmethath* was
located in the vicinity of Shechem (literally, 'before Shechem',
not necessarily *to the east of Shechem*). *Jashub* – the reading requires a slight textual emendation – is to be associated with the
modern village of Yāsūf located near the sources of *the gorge of
Kanah*. The text of verse 9 is corrupt and its meaning unclear.

10*b*. The phrase *and their boundary was the sea* should be
read with the sentence which follows. Manasseh's southern
boundary has already been described in verses 7–10*a*. The
purpose of verse 10*b* is to indicate her boundaries on the other
three sides. Literally, it reads: 'and the sea was their boundary
[i.e. on the west] and they reached Asher on the north and
Issachar on the east'. Obviously this summary of Manasseh's
remaining boundaries leaves some rather sizeable gaps.

11–13. Here again, as in 15: 63 and 16: 10, material from
the list of unconquered cities (Judg. 1: 21, 27–35) has been
incorporated into the description of the territorial allotments.
A problem for the editor arose in this case, however, since
the cities which the list associated with Manasseh were situated
on the southern edge of, and within, the Jezreel Valley – i.e.
territory which the boundary system seems to associate with
Issachar and Asher (see Josh. 19: 17–31 and Map 5). The vague
reference to the cities which Manasseh possessed *in Issachar
and Asher* but was unable to occupy may be an attempt to
reconcile this inconsistency, although it does not appear that
any of these cities was situated in Asher. Note that the tradition
reflected in Josh. 17: 16–18 also remembers conflict between
the Josephite tribes and the Canaanites of the Jezreel Valley.

The cities listed in verse 11 are precisely those mentioned in
Judg. 1: 27, with the exception that *En-dor* has been added

alongside *Dor* and a notation attached at the end of the list which states literally that 'the third [i.e. Dor, the third name in the list] is Naphath'. The Dor to which the list originally referred was probably not Naphath-Dor, however, but the Dor which was situated in the Jezreel Valley (see comment on 12: 23). ✳

THE SONS OF JOSEPH REQUEST MORE TERRITORY

14 The sons of Joseph appealed to Joshua and said, 'Why have you given us only one lot and one share as our patrimony? We are a numerous people; so far the LORD
15 has blessed us.' Joshua replied, 'If you are so numerous, go up into the forest in the territory of the Perizzites and the Rephaim and clear it for yourselves. You are their
16 near neighbours*a* in the hill-country of Ephraim.' The sons of Joseph said, 'The hill-country is not enough for us; besides, all the Canaanites have chariots of iron, those who inhabit the valley beside Beth-shean and its villages
17 and also those in the Vale of Jezreel.' Joshua replied to the tribes*b* of Joseph, that is Ephraim and Manasseh: 'You are a numerous people with great resources. You shall
18 not have one lot only. The hill-country is yours. It is forest land; clear it and it shall be yours to its furthest limits. The Canaanites may be powerful and equipped with chariots of iron, but you will be able to drive them out.'

✳ The Deuteronomistic editor seems to have conflated two different versions of an old tradition in this passage. The central theme of the tradition is a request for more territory on the part of the sons of Joseph. According to the version reflected

[a] You are...neighbours: *prob. rdg.; Heb. obscure.*   [b] *Lit.* house.

in verses 14–15, Joshua suggested that they clear the forests and thus utilize more fully the territory which already had been assigned to them. According to the other version, reflected primarily in verses 16–18, the sons of Joseph complained not only that the hill-country was too confining, but that they were meeting with resistance on the part of the Canaanites who inhabited the valleys of Beth-shean and Jezreel (see comment on 17: 11–13). Joshua's response is again that the house of Joseph should solve its own expansion problem by utilizing the hill-country to its furthest limits. He assures them, moreover, of victory over the Canaanites.

14. *only one lot and one share*: this passage and the opening phrase of 16: 1 treat the sons of Joseph as a single tribal unit which received a single portion. But the description of their allotment which follows 16: 1 assumes separate territorial assignments to Ephraim and Manasseh, and according to 17: 5–6 the Manassites alone received twelve shares. This apparent discrepancy is due to the fact that the traditions upon which the Deuteronomistic editor relied for his treatment of the Josephite tribes reflected different points of view (see comment on 14: 3–4).

15. *You are their near neighbours*: as the N.E.B. footnote indicates, the translation is an effort on the part of the N.E.B. to render meaningful an obscure Hebrew phrase. The N.E.B. rendering of the phrase presupposes the foregoing reference to the Perizzites and the Rephaim, which however is probably intrusive to the text, and in fact is missing in the Septuagint. The R.S.V. translation is less arbitrary and more easily justified on the basis of the context: 'The hill-country of Ephraim is too narrow for you.' *

THE ASSEMBLY AT SHILOH

The whole community of the Israelites met together at **18** Shiloh and established the Tent of the Presence there. The country now lay subdued at their feet, but there 2 remained seven tribes among the Israelites who had not yet taken possession of the patrimonies which would fall 3 to them. Joshua therefore said to them, 'How much longer will you neglect to take possession of the land which the LORD the God of your fathers has given you? 4 Appoint three men from each tribe whom I may send out to travel through the whole country. They shall make a register showing the patrimony suitable for each tribe, 5 and come back to me, and then it can be shared out among you in seven portions. Judah shall retain his boundary in the south, and the house of Joseph their 6 boundary in the north. You shall register the land in seven portions, bring the lists here, and I will cast lots for 7 you in the presence of the LORD our God. Levi has no share among you, because his share is the priesthood of the LORD; and Gad, Reuben, and the half tribe of Manasseh have each taken possession of their patrimony east of the Jordan, which Moses the servant of the LORD 8 gave them.' So the men set out on their journeys. Joshua ordered the emissaries to survey the country: 'Go through the whole country,' he said, 'survey it and return to me, and I will cast lots for you here before the LORD in Shiloh.' 9 So the men went and passed through the country; they registered it on a scroll, city by city, in seven portions, 10 and came to Joshua in the camp at Shiloh. Joshua cast lots for them in Shiloh before the LORD, and distributed the land there to the Israelites in their proper shares.

✷ Having assigned territory to the tribes of Judah and Joseph, Joshua assembles Israel at Shiloh and arranges for the allotment of territory to the remaining seven tribes: Benjamin, Simeon, Zebulon, Issachar, Asher, Naphtali and Dan. The procedure which he followed seems fair enough: a representative body (three men from each tribe) surveyed the land which had not yet been allotted, registered it city by city, and divided it into seven shares. Joshua, then, by casting lots, assigned the shares to the respective tribes. A detailed description of these allotments is provided in the remainder of ch. 18 and ch. 19.

1. The designation *Tent of the Presence* is one of the favourite expressions of the Priestly writer (see *Understanding the Old Testament* in this series esp. p. 158), but it rarely appears in the Deuteronomistic sections of the Old Testament. The only exceptions are this verse, Deut. 31: 14–15, and 1 Sam. 2: 22. Elsewhere in the book of Joshua the Ark of the Covenant symbolizes God's presence in Israel's camp (see comment on 3: 3). The rather surprising reference to the Tent of the Presence in this passage, plus the somewhat redundant style, suggests that the passage has been revised and expanded during the process of transmission at the hands of someone influenced by the Priestly tradition.

3. *How much longer will you neglect to take possession*: note the contrast between the tribes of Judah and Joseph, who are depicted as pressing Joshua for territorial assignments (14: 6–15; 17: 14–18), and the remaining seven tribes who are accused of neglecting to appropriate land even after the country 'lay subdued at their feet' (verse 1).

4. *Appoint three men from each tribe*: presumably the editor had in mind here only representatives of the seven tribes which had not yet received territorial allotments.

5. It makes sense to speak of *Judah...in the south, and the house of Joseph...in the north* from the perspective of Gilgal, which has been the scene of the Israelite camp heretofore in the book of Joshua since the crossing of the Jordan. It does not make sense from the perspective of Shiloh (verse 1), which is supposedly the scene of this final stage of the territorial distribution. Shiloh, in fact, lay within the territory which had already been assigned to Ephraim.

9. *the men...passed through the country*: again one would

139

presume that the editor had in mind only that territory which had not already been assigned to Judah and Joseph. The Hebrew term which is translated *scroll* simply indicates a written document, i.e. possibly, but not necessarily, a scroll. The registry was to be made *city by city*. Note that the three major sources upon which the Deuteronomistic editor based his description of the tribal allotments were city lists of various sorts. These were: (1) the boundary list which indicated the crucial points, mostly cities, on the lines between various tribes. This list probably dated from the period of the Judges (see comment on 15: 1–12). (2) The list of Judaean cities, which probably was an administrative document from the kingdom of Judah (see the general comments on 15: 20–62 and the comments on 18: 21–4, 25–8 and Map 3). (3) The list of unconquered cities (see comment on 15: 63). He may have had access also to city lists for the tribe of Simeon (see comment on 19: 1–9), and for the Galilean tribes (see comment on 19: 10–16). ✳

BENJAMIN'S LOT

11 This is the lot which fell to the tribe of the Benjamites family by family. The territory allotted to them lay
12 between the territory of Judah and Joseph. Their boundary at its northern corner starts from the Jordan; it goes up the slope on the north side of Jericho, continuing westwards into the hill-country, and its limit there is the
13 wilderness of Beth-aven. From there it runs on to Luz, to the southern slope of Luz, that is Bethel, and down to Ataroth-addar over the hill-country south of Lower
14 Beth-horon. The boundary then bends round at the west corner southwards from the hill-country above Beth-horon, and its limit is Kiriath-baal, that is Kiriath-jearim,
15 a city of Judah. This is the western side. The southern

side starts from the edge of Kiriath-jearim and ends*ᵃ* at
the spring of the waters of Nephtoah. It goes down to the 16
edge of the hill to the east of the Valley of Ben-hinnom,
north of the Vale of Rephaim, down the Valley of
Hinnom, to the southern slope of the Jebusites and so to
En-rogel. It then bends round north and comes out at 17
En-shemesh, goes on to the districts in front of the ascent
of Adummim and thence down to the Stone of Bohan
son of Reuben. It passes to the northern side of the slope 18
facing the Arabah and goes down to the Arabah, passing 19
the northern slope of Beth-hoglah, and its limit is the
northern inlet of the Dead Sea, at the southern mouth of
the Jordan. This forms the southern boundary. The 20
Jordan is the boundary on the east side. This is the patrimony of the Benjamites, the complete circuit of their
boundaries family by family.

The cities belonging to the tribe of the Benjamites 21
family by family are: Jericho, Beth-hoglah, Emek-keziz,
Beth-arabah, Zemaraim, Bethel, Avvim, Parah, Ophrah, 22, 23
Kephar-ammoni, Ophni, and Geba: twelve cities in all 24
with their hamlets. Gibeon, Ramah, Beeroth, Mizpah, 25, 26
Kephirah, Mozah, Rekem, Irpeel, Taralah, Zela, Eleph, 27, 28
Jebus,*ᵇ* that is Jerusalem, Gibeah, and Kiriath-jearim:*ᶜ*
fourteen cities in all with their hamlets. This is the patrimony of the Benjamites family by family.

☆ Benjamin received a very small share between the tribes
of Judah and Joseph. Verses 12–13 describe Benjamin's
northern (Ephraim's southern) boundary; verse 14, the western boundary; and verses 15–19, the southern (Judah's nor-

[a] *Prob. rdg.; Heb. adds* westwards and ends...
[b] *So Sept.; Heb.* the Jebusite.   [c] *So Sept.; Heb.* Kiriath.

thern) boundary. According to verse 20, a short section of the Jordan near Jericho served as the boundary on the east. The list of Benjamite cities in verses 21–8 is, as we have already noted, but a fragment of a more extensive list, the major portion of which has been incorporated into the description of Judah's tribal allotment (see comment on 15: 20–63). The original list included twelve subsections in all, each concluded with a sub-total and each corresponding to one of the administrative divisions of the kingdom of Judah (see Map 3). The Deuteronomistic editor has incorporated one of these subsections (verses 21–4, which corresponds to district XI) and the major portion of another (verses 25–8, which, with 15: 60, corresponds to district X) into his description of Benjamin's allotment, since the cities of these two subsections lay within traditional Benjamite territory.

12–13. Benjamin's northern boundary corresponds to Ephraim's southern boundary, which the editor has already described (see 16: 1–4). A note has been added – possibly by the Deuteronomistic editor, but more probably by a later scribe – which equates *Luz* with *Bethel*. The two are clearly viewed as separate sites in 16: 1–2, however, and Bethel appears there in the place of Beth-aven. Verse 13 should probably be emended slightly to read 'Ataroth-addar *to* the hill-country (mountain) south of Lower Beth-Horon'. Thus Benjamin's northern boundary began at the Jordan just north of Jericho, passed through the hill-country in the vicinity of Bethel and Ataroth-addar (see comment on 16: 1–4), and ended south of the Lower Beth-horon.

14. A more literal translation of this verse would indicate that the hill-country (or 'mountain') which marked Benjamin's north-western corner was actually located south of the Lower Beth-horon: 'The boundary then turns around at the west corner southwards, from the hill-country (mountain) over against Beth-horon on the south.' The notation which equates *Kiriath-baal* with *Kiriath-jearim, a city of Judah* has the character of a secondary gloss and may be an oversimplification

(see comment on 15: 6–11). The south-western corner of Benjamin's allotment was in any case near Kiriath-jearim.

15–19. This description of Benjamin's southern boundary duplicates almost word for word the description of Judah's northern boundary except that it is slightly abbreviated and it traces the line in the opposite direction (see comment on 15: 6–11).

21–4. The cities of district IX were located in the eastern hill-country, all of them some distance north and east of Jerusalem. The appearance of *Beth-hoglah* and *Beth-arabah* in this district is problematic in that Beth-arabah is also listed in district XII (15: 61). The two sites were near to each other, and Beth-arabah may have been situated even further north than Beth-hoglah.

Although the city list apparently originated as an administrative document for the kingdom of Judah, a number of the cities of district IX lay outside Judah, at least with respect to the lines as they were drawn originally after the division of Solomon's empire. *Bethel*, for example, served as one of the national sanctuaries of the northern kingdom during Jeroboam's reign (1 Kings 12: 29ff.). Yet the boundary between the two kingdoms changed from time to time. It has been pointed out, in fact, that the ninth district corresponds roughly to the territory which Abijah (about 908–905 B.C.) was able to wrest from Jeroboam during his latter years (2 Chron. 13: 19).

25–8. It is doubtful that Kiriath-baal and *Rabbah* alone formed a district (see 15: 60). More probably they belonged to the district which is represented by this second group of Benjamite cities. Verses 25–8 seem to overlap 15: 60 with regard to Kiriath-jearim. But this is not necessarily the case. On the one hand, the notation in 15: 60 which equates Kiriath-baal with Kiriath-jearim is a secondary gloss and possibly an oversimplification (see comment on 15: 6–11). The Hebrew text of 18: 28 is corrupt, on the other hand, and should probably be emended to read: 'Gibeath (i.e. the hill of) Kiriath-jearim'. This 'hill of Kiriath-jearim' is mentioned again in 1 Sam. 7: 1–2.

The note which identifies *Jebus* (literally 'the Jebusite') as *Jerusalem* is an intrusive element in the list, and the question of its accuracy has already been raised (see comments on 15: 6–11, 48–60, and 63). Besides the problems with this identification discussed above, it is doubtful that Jerusalem would have been listed in any one of the districts of the kingdom of Judah since it was the capital of the kingdom. And if it were included, surely it would not have been designated as 'the Jebusite' in an official administrative document. Jebusites did control Jerusalem prior to its conquest by David. But the Egyptian records confirm that the city was already called 'Jerusalem' during the Bronze Age and it is called that consistently throughout the Old Testament. ✷

SIMEON'S LOT

19 The second lot cast was for Simeon, the tribe of the Simeonites family by family. Their patrimony was in-
2 cluded in that of Judah. For their patrimony they had
3, 4 Beersheba,*a* Moladah, Hazar-shual, Balah, Ezem, Eltolad,
5 Bethul, Hormah, Ziklag, Beth-marcaboth, Hazar-susah,
6 Beth-lebaoth, and Sharuhen: in all, thirteen cities and
7 their hamlets. They had Ain, Rimmon, Ether, and Ashan:
8 four cities and their hamlets, all the hamlets round these cities as far as Baalath-beer, Ramath-negeb. This was the
9 patrimony of the tribe of Simeon family by family. The patrimony of the Simeonites was part of the land allotted to the men of Judah, because their share was larger than they needed. The Simeonites therefore had their patrimony within the territory of Judah.

[*a*] *Prob. rdg., cp. 1 Chr. 4: 28; Heb. adds* and Sheba.

✻ Simeon is given an allotment within the territorial bounds of Judah. All the cities listed are located in the Negeb. The list is duplicated in 1 Chron. 4: 28–33.

1. *Their patrimony was included in that of Judah*: the Deutero-nomistic editor justifies this allotment in verse 9 on the grounds that Judah's share 'was larger than they needed'. Actually the tribe of Simeon plays a very elusive role in the Old Testament narratives and may have been absorbed into Judah quite early in Israel's history.

2–8. It is questionable whether the editor had any specific information in his sources concerning Simeon's allotment. The boundary list which he otherwise relies upon throughout his description of the allotments west of the Jordan apparently did not take Simeon into consideration. Most of the cities which he assigns to Simeon here have appeared already in the list of Judahite cities. Some scholars hold, therefore, that the Deuteronomistic editor constructed this Simeonite city list artificially, deriving most of the names from the Judahite list. Others contend, however, that he had access to an independent Simeonite list with which he expanded the Judahite list.

Recent archaeological excavations at *Beersheba* indicate that it was an important fortress city on Judah's southern frontier during the period of the divided kingdom. David was given *Ziklag* by Achish, the Philistine king of Gath, and the city played an important role in his rise to power (1 Sam. 27: 6; 30). *Sharuhen* is mentioned in the Egyptian records as the town to which the Hyksos retreated after their expulsion from Egypt. ✻

ZEBULUN'S LOT

The third lot fell to the Zebulunites family by family. 10
The boundary of their patrimony extended to Shadud.[a]
Their boundary went up westwards as far as Maralah 11
and touched Dabbesheth and the gorge east of Jokneam.

[a] *Prob. rdg.; Heb.* Sarid (*similarly in verse 12*).

12 It turned back from Shadud eastwards towards the sunrise
up to the border of Kisloth-tabor, on to Daberath and up
13 to Japhia. From there it crossed eastwards towards the
sunrise to Gath-hepher, to Ittah-kazin, out to Rimmon,
14 and bent round[a] to Neah. The northern boundary went
round to Hannathon, and its limits were the Valley of
15 Jiphtah-el, Kattath, Nahalal, Shimron, Idalah, and Beth-
16 lehem: twelve cities in all with their hamlets. These cities
and their hamlets were the patrimony of Zebulun family
by family.

✻ Zebulun was a small tribe which occupied a southern
branch of the Galilean mountains. It is closely associated in
the biblical texts with Issachar, whose territory lay to the
south-east and who shared a sanctuary with Zebulun on
Mount Tabor.

The descriptions of the territorial allotments of the Galilean
tribes and Dan are similar in that they combine brief boundary
notations with lists of cities. These descriptions, as in the case
of Zebulun, may consist largely of boundary points with
only a few cities listed in unbroken sequence; or, as in the
cases of Issachar, Naphtali and Dan, they may appear to be
nothing more than city lists, rarely interrupted with references
to the boundaries. In each of these cases, however, the
Deuteronomistic editor probably derived much of his information from the same boundary tradition which he relied
upon in connection with the tribes of the central hill-country.
This source was essentially a city list, as we have already seen
(see comment on 15: 1–12). The editor himself probably
supplied the connecting verbs, prepositions, etc. He has done
this less consistently for the Galilean tribes and Dan. Not all
the cities listed for these remaining tribes can be conceived as
boundary points, however. The editor also drew upon other

[a] and bent round: *prob. rdg.; Heb.* which stretched.

146

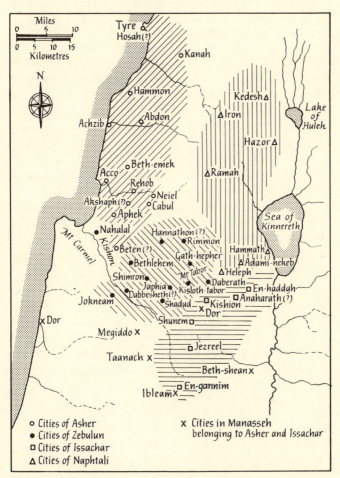

Cities of Asher
Cities of Zebulun
Cities of Issachar
Cities of Naphtali

× Cities in Manasseh
belonging to Asher and Issachar

5. Tribal boundaries in Galilee (19: 10–39). Cities and their villages which Manasseh possessed 'in Issachar and Asher' (17: 11–13) are indicated by a cross.

sources, such as the list of unconquered cities (see comment on 15: 63).

11–12. The boundary points for Zebulun which can be located with any degree of certainty were situated in the lower Galilean hills (see Map 5 and Gazetteer). The boundary is traced from *Shadud* westward to *the gorge east of* (over against) *Jokneam*, and then eastward by way of *Kisloth-tabor* and *Daberath* to *Japhia*. Jokneam is to be identified with Tell Qeimūn near present-day Yokne'am; thus the gorge probably was that of the Kishon which flows into the Mediterranean Sea near Haifa. The ancient name 'Japhia' is no doubt pre-served in that of present-day Yāfā, but seems out of place at this point in the boundary.

13–14. The text of these two verses is awkwardly worded. Apparently they are designed to describe Zebulun's eastern boundary.

With the valley of *Jiphtah-el* we have reached Zebulun's western side (see 19: 27). ✳

ISSACHAR'S LOT

17 The fourth lot cast was for the sons of Issachar family
18 by family. Their boundary included Jezreel, Kesulloth,
19, 20 Shunem, Hapharaim, Shion, Anaharath, Rabbith, Ki-
21 shion, Ebez, Remeth, En-gannim, En-haddah, and Beth-
22 pazzez. The boundary touched Tabor, Shahazumah, and Beth-shemesh, and its limit was the Jordan: sixteen cities
23 with their hamlets. This was the patrimony of the tribe of the sons of Issachar family by family, both cities and hamlets.

✳ Only a few of Issachar's cities can be located geographically with any degree of certainty (see Map 5 and Gazetteer). From those which can be located, it is apparent that Issachar occupied the territory immediately to the south-east of Zebulun. The northern boundary would have been roughly a line extending between Mount Tabor and the southern end of the Sea of Kinnereth (Galilee). The eastern boundary would have been the Jordan. *Kesulloth* is identical with Kisloth-tabor, which apparently was located on the Issachar side of the Issachar–Zebulun boundary (see comment on 19: 11–12). ✶

ASHER'S LOT

The fifth lot cast was for the tribe of the Asherites 24 family by family. Their boundary included Helkath, Hali, 25 Beten, Akshaph, Alammelech, Amad, and Mishal; it 26 touched Carmel on the west and the swamp of Libnath. It then turned back towards the east to Beth-dagon, 27 touched Zebulun and the Valley of Jiphtah-el on the north at Beth-emek and Neiel, and reached Cabul on its northern side, and Abdon,[a] Rehob, Hammon, and Kanah 28 as far as Greater Sidon. The boundary turned at Ramah, 29 going as far as the fortress city of Tyre, and then back again to Hosah, and its limits to the west were Mehalbeh,[b] Achzib, Acco,[c] Aphek, and Rehob: twenty-two cities in 30 all with their hamlets. This was the patrimony of the tribe 31 of Asher family by family, these cities and their hamlets.

✶ According to this passage, Asher received a rather large territorial allotment: apparently all the territory west of Zebulun and Naphtali, extending from the Carmel mountains in the south to the frontier of Sidonian territory in the north. The Asherites probably in fact settled primarily on the western slopes of the Galilean highlands, with some intermingling among the Canaanite city states below. According

[a] *So some MSS.*, *cp. 21: 30; 1 Chr. 6: 74; others* Ebron.
[b] *In Judg. 1: 31* Ahlab.
[c] Mehalbeh...Acco: *prob. rdg.; Heb.* from the district of Achzib and Ummah.

to the list of unconquered cities in Judg. 1: 31–2, 'Asher did not drive out the inhabitants of Acco and Sidon, of Ahlab, Achzib, Helbah, Aphik and Rehob. Thus the Asherites lived among the Canaanite inhabitants and did not drive them out' (see comment on 15: 63).

25–6a. These seven cities were probably situated on or near the plain of Acco, which would have *touched Carmel on the west*. The reference to *the swamp of Libnath* is rather awkwardly attached, and the translation, 'swamp', is open to question.

27–8. Asher's eastern boundary is described. *Beth-dagon* cannot be located, but we have encountered *the Valley of Jiphtah-el* already in connection with Zebulun's western boundary. *Cabul* lay further north, as did the four cities whose names follow. *Greater Sidon* probably refers more generally to the frontier of the territory dominated by Sidon than to the city itself; that is, Asher's eastern boundary extended north until it reached Sidonian territory (see 11: 8 and 13: 6).

29. Literally, the verse reads: 'The boundary turns at Ramah, and as far as the fortress city of Tyre, and the boundary turns to Hosah, and it ends in the sea.' The reference to *the fortress city of Tyre* prior to *Hosah* is problematic, since Tyre itself was situated on an off-shore island of the Mediterranean coast, and there is some reason to believe that Hosah was an on-shore suburb of the same city (see Gazetteer). The N.E.B. attempts to solve this problem by avoiding the reference to the sea and rendering the crucial phrase, *and its limits to the west were Mehalbeh, Achzib...* But the five cities whose names follow have nothing to do with Asher's boundary; the editor derived their names from the list of unconquered cities (see Judg. 1: 31–2). *

NAPHTALI'S LOT

³² The sixth lot cast was for the sons of Naphtali family
³³ by family. Their boundary started from Heleph and[a] from Elon-bezaanannim and ran past Adami-nekeb and Jabneel

[a] So Sept.; Heb. om.

as far as Lakkum, and its limit was the Jordan. The boun- 34
dary turned back westwards to Aznoth-tabor and from
there on to Hukok. It touched Zebulun on the south,
Asher on the west, and the low-lying land by the Jordan
on the east. Their fortified cities were Ziddim, Zer, 35
Hammath, Rakkath, Kinnereth, Adamah, Ramah, Hazor, 36
Kedesh, Edrei, En-hazor, Iron, Migdal-el, Horem, Beth- 37, 38
anath, and Beth-shemesh: nineteen cities with their hamlets. This was the patrimony of the tribe of Naphtali family 39
by family, both cities and hamlets.

✻ This description of the territory assigned to Naphtali is
difficult to follow geographically, since few of the sites can
be located with confidence and since the text of verse 34*b* is
corrupt. Apparently the remainder of the Galilean territory
is assigned to Naphtali, specifically the western part of the
Jordan Valley from the lake of Huleh in the north to the
southern end of the Sea of Kinnereth.

33–4*a*. These two verses seem to describe a single east–west
boundary, beginning in the middle. Verse 33 gives the eastern
segment of the line from *Heleph* and *Elon-bezaanannim* (or
'the Oak at Zaanannim') to the Jordan; verse 34 describes
the western segment from Heleph/Zaanannim to *Hukok*.
Unfortunately, none of the sites designated along the boundary
can be located with any certainty. Indeed, there has been some
difference of opinion among scholars whether this line bounded Naphtali on the north or on the south. *Aznoth-tabor* must
have been in the vicinity of Mount Tabor, however, establishing the line as the southern boundary. Those who take it
as the northern boundary do so largely on the basis of Judg.
4: 11, which places Elon-bezaanannim near Kedesh, which
they associate in turn with Tell Qades in the Huleh valley.
But the reference in Judg. 4: 11 is probably to another Kedesh
(see 'Kedesh' in the Gazetteer).

34 *b*. *and the low-lying land by the Jordan on the east*: the text is corrupt. One would expect a reference to Issachar at this point.

35–8. Although it is claimed that Naphtali touched Asher on the west, the core of Naphtalite settlement seems to have been on the eastern slopes of the Galilean hill-country and along the valley, from the lake of Huleh to the southern end of the Sea of Kinnereth (Galilee). Deut. 33: 23 associates Naphtali with Kinnereth, and the cities listed (which can be located with any degree of certainty) lie primarily in that area. ✶

DAN'S LOT

40 The seventh lot cast was for the tribe of the sons of
41 Dan family by family. The boundary of their patrimony
42 was Zorah, Eshtaol, Ir-shemesh, Shaalabbin, Aijalon,
43, 44 Jithlah, Elon, Timnah, Ekron, Eltekeh, Gibbethon,
45, 46 Baalath, Jehud, Bene-berak, Gath-rimmon; and on the
47 west Jarkon was the boundary[a] opposite Joppa. But the Danites, when they lost this territory, marched against Leshem, attacked it and captured it. They put its people to the sword, occupied it and settled in it; and they
48 renamed the place Dan after their ancestor Dan. This was the patrimony of the tribe of the sons of Dan family by family, these cities and their hamlets.

✶ Dan is assigned territory in the Shephelah and coastal plain north of Judah's boundary, extending as far as Joppa and the river Jarkon.

41–6. Most of the cities in this list were located on or near the boundaries of the territory allotted to Dan (see Map 4); thus the Deuteronomistic editor was probably relying heavily at this point on the old boundary source (see comments on

[a] and on . . . boundary: *so* Sept. ; *Heb*. Me-jarkon and Rakkon were on the boundary.

15: 1–12 and 19: 10–16). *Ir-shemesh* (i.e. Beth-Shemesh), *Timnah, Ekron* and *Baalath* have been listed already as border points in the description of Judah's northern boundary (15: 10–11). Located on or near the boundary which Dan supposedly would have shared with Ephraim, tracing the line northward from Beth-shemesh, were *Zorah, Eshtaol, Aijalon* and *Shaalabbin. Jehud, Bene-berak,* and *Gath-rimmon* would have marked Dan's northern frontier.

47. The Danites, however, were unable to appropriate this allotted territory. According to Judg. 1: 34–5 'The Amorites pressed the Danites back into the hill-country and did not allow them to come down into the Vale. The Amorites held their ground in Mount Heres and in Aijalon and Shaalbim, but the tribes of Joseph increased their pressure on them until they reduced them to forced labour.' The narratives concerning Samson (Judg. 13–16) reflect a situation in which the Danites are oppressed by the Philistines, whose territory their allotment also overlapped. The Danite migration northward and the conquest of *Leshem,* briefly noted here, is recounted in Judg. 18. *

JOSHUA'S SPECIAL ALLOTMENT

So the Israelites finished allocating the land and marking 49 out its frontiers; and they gave Joshua son of Nun a patrimony within their territory. They followed the 50 commands of the LORD and gave him the city for which he asked, Timnath-serah[a] in the hill-country of Ephraim, and he rebuilt the city and settled in it.

These are the patrimonies which Eleazar the priest and 51 Joshua son of Nun and the heads of families assigned by lot to the Israelite tribes at Shiloh before the LORD at the entrance of the Tent of the Presence. Thus they completed the distribution of the land.

[a] *In Judg. 2: 9* Timnath-heres.

* The conclusion of the assignment of territory to the secular tribes is marked by a special allotment to Joshua in the hill-country of Ephraim. Judg. 2:9 may have preserved an older form of the name of Joshua's city, i.e. 'Timnath-heres', which means 'portion of the sun'. The name seems to be preserved in that of Khirbet Tibneh, which is located about 27 kilometres (16 miles) south-west of Shechem. *

THE CITIES OF REFUGE

20 1,2 The LORD spoke to Joshua and commanded him to say this to the Israelites: 'You must now appoint your cities of refuge, of which I spoke to you through Moses.
3 They are to be places where the homicide, the man who kills another inadvertently without intent, may take sanctuary. You shall single them out as cities of refuge
4 from the vengeance of the dead man's next-of-kin. When a man takes sanctuary in one of these cities, he shall halt at the entrance of the city gate and state his case in the hearing of the elders of that city; if they admit him into the city, they shall grant him a place where he may live
5 as one of themselves. When the next-of-kin comes in pursuit, they shall not surrender him: he struck down his fellow without intent and had not previously been at
6 enmity with him. The homicide may stay in that city until he stands trial before the community. On the death of the ruling high priest, he may return to the city and
7 home from which he has fled.' They dedicated Kedesh in Galilee in the hill-country of Naphtali, Shechem in the hill-country of Ephraim, and Kiriath-arba, that is Hebron,
8 in the hill-country of Judah. Across the Jordan eastwards from Jericho they appointed these cities: from the tribe

of Reuben, Bezer-in-the-wilderness on the tableland, from the tribe of Gad, Ramoth in Gilead, and from the tribe of Manasseh, Golan in Bashan. These were the 9 appointed cities where any Israelite or any alien residing among them might take sanctuary. They were intended for any man who killed another inadvertently, to ensure that no one should die at the hand of the next-of-kin until he had stood his trial before the community.

✵ This passage assumes that, in the case of murder, it was the responsibility of the victim's next-of-kin to avenge the deed by taking the murderer's life. Six cities were set aside as places of asylum, however, for anyone who killed another by accident.

2. *of which I spoke to you through Moses*: a more detailed explanation of the city-of-refuge system is provided in Num. 35: 9–34 (see also Exod. 21: 12–14 and Deut. 19: 1–13) where it is reported as a commandment from God to Moses. Otherwise the city-of-refuge system is not reflected in any of the biblical narratives and its historicity is thus open to question. Scholars who see it as an historical rather than an ideal system tend to associate it with either David's reign or Josiah's reform.

3. *next-of-kin*: literally 'avenger of blood'. According to the traditional saying in Gen. 9: 6,

> He that sheds the blood of man,
> for that man his blood shall be shed;
> for in the image of God
> has God made man.

This saying refers, of course, not merely to the shedding of human blood, but to murder in general. Accordingly, a murdered victim's next-of-kin whose duty it was to avenge the death was referred to as the 'avenger of blood'.

4–6. Except for the phrase, *until he stands trial before the*

community, these three verses are absent from several of the
Septuagint manuscripts and may have been introduced secondarily on the basis of Num. 35: 9–34. Moreover, this phrase
is somewhat inconsistent with the remainder of verse 6.
According to the latter (as in Num. 35), it was *the death of the
ruling high priest* rather than a second trial which marked the
end of an accidental manslayer's period of asylum. The view
reflected seems to be that the taking of a human life, accidental
or not, imposed a guilt which could be expiated only by
another death. Normally, it was the murderer who paid with
his own life at the hand of the victim's next-of-kin. In the
case of an accidental homicide, however, the death of the
ruling high priest apparently served as a substitute.

7–8. The six cities of refuge were spaced relatively evenly,
three on either side of the Jordan (see Map 6). At least one of
the cities would have been within reach, therefore, regardless of
where the fatal accident occurred. The reading *Across the Jordan
eastwards from Jericho* assumes a small textual emendation. ✻

SPECIAL ARRANGEMENTS FOR THE LEVITES

21 The heads of the Levite families approached Eleazar
the priest and Joshua son of Nun and the heads of the
² families of the tribes of Israel. They came before them at
Shiloh in the land of Canaan and said, 'The LORD gave
his command through Moses that we were to receive
cities to live in, together with the common land belonging
³ to them for our cattle.' The Israelites therefore gave part
of their patrimony to the Levites, the following cities
with their common land, according to the command of
the LORD.

⁴ This is the territory allotted to the Kohathite family:
those Levites who were descended from Aaron the priest
received thirteen cities chosen by lot from the tribes of

Judah, Simeon, and Benjamin; the rest of the Kohathites 5
were allotted family by family*ᵃ* ten cities from the tribes
of Ephraim, Dan, and half Manasseh.

The Gershonites were allotted family by family thirteen 6
cities from the tribes of Issachar, Asher, Naphtali, and the
half tribe of Manasseh in Bashan.

The Merarites were allotted*ᵇ* family by family twelve 7
cities from the tribes of Reuben, Gad, and Zebulun.

So the Israelites gave the Levites these cities with their 8
common land, allocating them by lot as the LORD had
commanded through Moses.

✵ The Deuteronomistic editor has reminded his readers
several times that the Levites did not receive a territorial
allotment as such, but that special arrangements were made
in their case (13: 14, 33; 14: 4; 18: 7). Ch. 21 explains these
arrangements in some detail. The Levites were assigned
certain cities throughout the land where they could live and
graze their cattle in the surrounding pastures.

1. *The heads of the Levite families*: three Levitical families are
recognized here and elsewhere in the later strata of the Old
Testament: Kohathites, Gershonites, and Merarites. It is
assumed that these three families descended from Levi, one
of the twelve sons of Jacob, and that they were set apart as
cultic leaders because of the religious loyalty which they
demonstrated at the time of the exodus from Egypt. When
one explores behind the latest strata of the Old Testament,
however, it becomes increasingly apparent that this is an
oversimplified view of their origin. If the Levites did originate
as a secular tribe, persons of various tribal origins were
absorbed into their ranks from time to time. Some scholars

[a] family by family: *prob. rdg.; Heb.* from the families (*similarly in
verse 6*).
[b] were allotted: *so Sept.: Heb. om.*

argue that the term 'Levite' originally pertained to cultic office and function rather than to family origin.

2. *The LORD gave his command through Moses*: a more detailed (although clearly ideal) statement regarding the Levitical holdings in these cities is provided in Num. 35: 1–8, recorded as a commandment from God to Moses.

4–8. *those Levites who were descended from Aaron* are treated separately from the other Kohathites. Thus, while the editor recognizes three extended families among the Levites, he assigns the cities in four categories: the (Kohathite) descendants of Aaron received thirteen cities in Judah, Simeon, and Benjamin (see verses 9–19); the rest of the Kohathites received ten cities in Ephraim, Dan and Manasseh west of the Jordan (see verses 20–6); the Gershonites received thirteen cities in Issachar, Asher, Naphtali, and Manasseh east of the Jordan (see verses 27–33); and the Merarites received twelve cities in Reuben, Gad, and Zebulun (see verses 34–40). ✳

THE LEVITICAL CITIES

9 The Israelites designated the following cities out of the
10 tribes of Judah and Simeon for those sons of Aaron who were of the Kohathite families of the Levites, because
11 their lot came out first. They gave them Kiriath-arba (Arba was the father of Anak), that is Hebron, in the hill-
12 country of Judah, and the common land round it, but they gave the open country near the city, and its hamlets, to Caleb son of Jephunneh as his patrimony.

13[a]   To the sons of Aaron the priest they gave Hebron, a
14 city of refuge for the homicide, Libnah, Jattir, Eshtemoa,
15,16 Holon, Debir, Ashan,[b] Juttah, and Beth-shemesh, each with its common land: nine cities from these two tribes.

[a] *Verses 13–39: cp. 1 Chr. 6: 57–81.*
[b] *Prob. rdg., cp. 1 Chr. 6: 59; Heb.* Ain.

They also gave cities from the tribe of Benjamin, Gibeon, 17
Geba, Anathoth, and Almon, each with its common land: 18
four cities. The number of the cities with their common 19
land given to the sons of Aaron the priest was thirteen.

The cities which the rest of the Kohathite families of 20
the Levites received by lot were from the tribe of
Ephraim. They gave them Shechem, a city of refuge for 21
the homicide, in the hill-country of Ephraim, Gezer,
Kibzaim, and Beth-horon, each with its common land: 22
four cities. From the tribe of Dan, they gave them 23
Eltekeh, Gibbethon, Aijalon, and Gath-rimmon, each 24
with its common land: four cities. From the half tribe 25
of Manasseh, they gave them Taanach and Gath-rimmon,
each with its common land: two cities. The number of 26
the cities belonging to the rest of the Kohathite families
with their common land was ten.

The Gershonite families of the Levites received, out of 27
the share of the half tribe of Manasseh, Golan in Bashan,
a city of refuge for the homicide, and Be-ashtaroth,[a] each
with its common land: two cities. From the tribe of 28
Issachar they received Kishon, Daberah, Jarmuth,[b] and 29
En-gannim, each with its common land: four cities. From 30
the tribe of Asher they received Mishal, Abdon, Helkath, 31
and Rehob, each with its common land: four cities. From 32
the tribe of Naphtali they received Kedesh in Galilee, a
city of refuge for the homicide, Hammoth-dor, and
Kartan, each with its common land: three cities. The 33
number of the cities of the Gershonite families with their
common land was thirteen.

[a] *Prob. rdg.; Heb.* Be-ashtarah.
[b] *Or, with Sept.,* Remeth, *cp. 19: 21.*

34 From the tribe of Zebulun the rest of the Merarite
35 families of the Levites received Jokneam, Kartah, Rimmon,*[a]* and Nahalal, each with its common land: four
36 cities. East of the Jordan at Jericho,*[b]* from the tribe of
Reuben they were given Bezer-in-the-wilderness on the
tableland,*[c]* a city of refuge for the homicide, Jahaz,
37 Kedemoth, and Mephaath, each with its common land:
38 four cities. From the tribe of Gad they received Ramoth
in Gilead, a city of refuge for the homicide, Mahanaim,
39 Heshbon, and Jazer, each with its common land: four
40 cities in all. Twelve cities in all fell by lot to the rest of the
Merarite families of the Levites.

41   The cities of the Levites within the Israelite patrimonies
numbered forty-eight in all, with their common land.
42 Each city had its common land round it, and it was the
same for all of them.

✻ The Levitical cities are listed and assigned. A slightly
different version of the same list is recorded in 1 Chron. 6.

Two characteristics of the list led many earlier scholars to
conclude that the system of Levitical cities was an ideal
arrangement with little or no historical basis. On the one hand,
the list is highly schematic, four cities listed for each tribe.
The only exceptions, Judah and Naphtali, offset each other
and probably are to be attributed to secondary changes in the
text (see comment on verses 11–12). On the other hand, the
list presupposes rather extensive territory for Israel, more
than her kings were normally able to control. Other factors,
however, have led an increasing number of scholars in recent
years to place more confidence in the list's historical authen-
ticity: (1) Israel did control the territory presupposed by the

[a] *Prob. rdg., cp. 19: 13; 1 Chr. 6: 77; Heb.* Dimnah.
[b] East...Jericho: *so Sept.; Heb. om.*
[c] Bezer...tableland: *so Sept.; Heb.* Bezer.

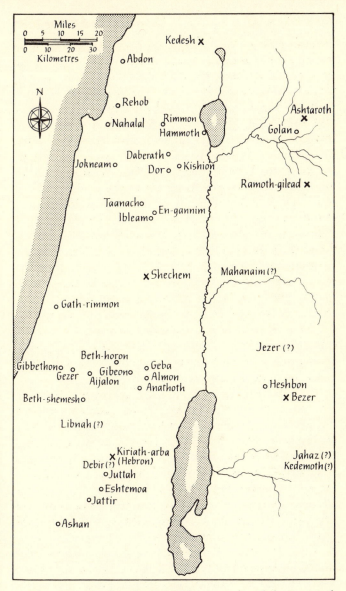

6. The cities of refuge (indicated by a cross) and the Levitical cities. See Gazetteer.

list during King David's reign. (2) The cities which can be located are not as evenly spaced as one would expect if the list were entirely ideal. There is a noticeable tendency, in fact, for them to be situated in frontier regions and in areas which remained outside Israelite control prior to the conquests of Saul and David. (3) The Chronicler contends that David charged the Levites with administrative as well as cultic responsibilities. We read in 1 Chron. 26: 29–32, for example, that from the Levitical family of Izhar, 'Kenaniah and his sons acted as clerks and magistrates in the secular affairs of Israel.' Of the Levitical family of Hashabiah which dwelt at Hebron, we are told further that seventeen hundred men of ability 'had the oversight of Israel west of the Jordan, both in the work of the LORD and in the service of the king'. These factors seem to suggest, in short, that the Levitical city system was an administrative arrangement initiated by King David for the governing of his newly expanded kingdom. This conclusion does not preclude the possibility, of course, that the list as it stands now is somewhat artificial. The twelve-tribe scheme seems at any rate to have been superimposed upon it, and an effort to emphasize the completeness of Israel's possession of the land may also have been operative.

11–12. With the exception of Judah/Simeon and Naphtali, a pattern of four Levitical cities per tribe obtains throughout the list. Nine cities are listed for Judah and Simeon and three for Naphtali. But in spite of the fact that these two exceptions offset each other and allow for the grand total of forty-eight cities in all (verse 41), both probably represent late changes in the text. The fact that *Kiriath-arba* does not appear in the Chronicler's version of the list suggests that it was introduced into the Joshua version secondarily. This was probably done on the basis of the list of refuge cities in the preceding chapter; the other five cities of refuge having already been included among the Levitical cities. Hammoth-dor, on the other hand, which is listed for Naphtali, probably should be read as two different names: Hammoth and Dor (see comment below).

If Kiriath-arba is intrusive to the list, then the same must be said for the series of notations associated with it – i.e. the explanation of the name, its identification as Hebron, the reference to the Calebites to whom Kiriath-arba had been assigned, and the observation that Hebron was a city of refuge. All of this information has been introduced already (14: 13-15; 15: 13; 20: 7).

Map 6 includes the Levitical cities which can be located with some certainty and indicates those which doubled as cities of refuge.

9-19. *cities out of the tribes of Judah and Simeon for. . .the Kohathite families* (descendants of Aaron): with the exception of *Holon* (verse 15), all of these cities can be located with some certainty. One is tempted to associate Holon with Khirbet 'Alīn on the western edge of the Judaean hill-country, but to do so would place it outside the fifth administrative district of the kingdom of Judah (see 15: 15 and Map 3 on p. 126).

20-6. Cities out of the tribes of *Ephraim, Dan*, and *Manasseh* (west of the Jordan) assigned to *the rest of the Kohathite families*: *Kibzaim* (verse 22) appears nowhere else in the Old Testament, and there is no evidence available regarding its location. This reading is preferable to that of the Chronicler's version of the Levitical city list, however, which introduces 'Jokmeam' at this point rather than among the cities of Zebulun (see verse 34). Note that *Beth-horon* (verse 22) is listed without any indication as to whether it is Upper or Lower Beth-horon. The Chronicler correctly records 'Bileam' (i.e. Ibleam) rather than *Gath-rimmon* for the second Manassite city (verse 25). The latter name has apparently been transferred by scribal carelessness from verse 24.

27-33. Cities out of *Manasseh* (Transjordan), *Issachar, Asher*, and *Naphtali* assigned to *the Gershonite families*: if *Golan* (verse 27) is to be associated with Saḥm el-Jōlān, as seems quite likely, then it stood near Ashtaroth. The next name which appears in the list, 'Be-ashtarah' according to the Hebrew text, seems to be a corruption of Ashtaroth. Note that the

Chronicler's version reads 'Ashtaroth'. The preposition 'Be' in Hebrew means 'in'. Thus the variant reading in Joshua may have originated when a scribe took the text to mean 'Golan in (or near) Ashtaroth'. *Hammoth-dor* of Naphtali (verse 32) should be read as two different names: 'Hammoth' and 'Dor'. This Dor is probably identical with the one listed in 12: 23 and 17: 11, regardless of the fact that 17: 11 seems to place it in Issachar. The territories of Naphtali and Issachar adjoined each other, and if Dor was situated on or near the boundary it could have been associated with either. Note the similar situation with regard to the cities of Dan (19: 41–3) – i.e. several of these Danite cities also appear in the description of Judah's border (15: 10–12). *Jarmuth* in Issachar (verse 29), *Mishal* (verse 30) and *Helkath* in Asher (verse 31) and *Kartan* in Naphtali (verse 32) cannot be located. Jarmuth ('Ramoth' in the Chronicler's version of the list) is probably the same as 'Remeth' in 19: 21.

34–40. Cities out of *Zebulun, Reuben,* and *Gad* assigned to *the rest of the Merarite families*: *Jokneam* (verse 34; 'Jokmeam' in 1 Kings 4: 12 and 1 Chron. 6: 68) has already appeared in the description of Zebulun's boundary (19: 11), although with the implication that it lay just outside Zebulun's limits. *Kartah* in Zebulun (verse 34; possibly confused with 'Kartan' in verse 32) and *Mephaath* in Reuben (verse 37) cannot be located. ✳

'THE LORD'S PROMISES...ALL CAME TRUE'

43 Thus the LORD gave Israel all the land which he had sworn to give to their forefathers; they occupied it and
44 settled in it. The LORD gave them security on every side as he had sworn to their forefathers. Of all their enemies not a man could withstand them; the LORD delivered
45 all their enemies into their hands. Not a word of the LORD's promises to the house of Israel went unfulfilled; they all came true.

✳ With this brief paragraph the Deuteronomistic historian concludes and summarizes the story which began in ch. 1. The conquest of the land has been completed. As in his other summaries (cp. 9: 1–2; 10: 40–3), this statement goes beyond the sum of the individual reports. He explicitly affirms not only that all the enemies had been dispatched but also that 'all the land' had been 'occupied' and 'settled'. But earlier (13: 1–6) he had taken note of the unconquered territory. Furthermore, in the book of Judges he will modify this generalization, pointing out that the LORD allowed some of the Canaanites to remain 'as a means of testing' Israel (cp. Judg. 2: 16 – 3: 6). The paragraph is a concise summary of the main theological affirmation of the book: the promises to the patriarchs reported in the book of Genesis have been fulfilled; the LORD has given their descendants the land. While the name of Joshua is not mentioned here, it will become painfully clear in the subsequent chapters of the Deuteronomistic history (cp. Judg. 2: 6–15) that the period of the LORD's unqualified help will not extend beyond the lifetime of Joshua.

44. *security*: see comments on 1: 13, 15. ✳

THE RETURN OF THE TRANSJORDANIAN TRIBES

At that time Joshua summoned the Reubenites, the **22** Gadites, and the half tribe of Manasseh, and said to them, 2 'You have observed all the commands of Moses the servant of the LORD, and you have obeyed me in all the commands that I too have laid upon you. All this 3 time you have not deserted your brothers; up to this day you have diligently observed the charge laid on you by the LORD your God. And now that the LORD your God 4 has given your brothers security as he promised them, you may turn now and go to your homes in your own land, the land which Moses the servant of the LORD gave

5 you east of the Jordan. But take good care to keep the commands and the law which Moses the servant of the LORD gave you: to love the LORD your God; to conform to his ways; to observe his commandments; to hold fast to him; to serve him with your whole heart and soul.'

6 Joshua blessed them and dismissed them; and they went

7–8 to their homes. He sent them home with his blessing, and with these words: 'Go to your homes richly laden, with great herds, with silver and gold, copper and iron, and with large stores of clothing. See that you share with your kinsmen the spoil you have taken from your enemies.'

Moses had given territory to one half of the tribe of Manasseh in Bashan, and Joshua gave territory to the other half west of the Jordan among their kinsmen.

✷ With the possible exception of verses 7–8, this entire section – like the previous paragraph – stems from the pen of the Deuteronomistic historian. He resumes and concludes the theme he initiated in 1: 12–18 (see notes). Joshua addresses the two-and-a-half Transjordanian tribes, acknowledging their obedience to the LORD's orders that they assist in the capture of Palestine and dismissing them with his blessing to return to their own territory. He includes the admonition that they remain faithful to the LORD and his law. The special attention to these tribes was necessary in order to maintain and emphasize that the conquest was the work of all Israel, operating in unison under Joshua.

7–8. The N.E.B. has rearranged the order of sentences in these verses. The reference to *the spoil* is consistent with some of the war stories (e.g. 8: 26; 11: 14) but against the rule of the holy war expressed in 6: 18–19 (see comment). ✷

THE TRANSJORDANIAN TRIBES BUILD AN ALTAR

So the Reubenites, the Gadites, and the half tribe of 9
Manasseh left the rest of the Israelites and went from
Shiloh in Canaan on their way into Gilead, the land which
belonged to them according to the decree of the LORD
given through Moses. When these tribes came to Geliloth 10
by the Jordan,[a] they built a great altar there by the river
for all to see. The Israelites heard that the Reubenites, 11
the Gadites, and the half tribe of Manasseh had built the
altar facing the land of Canaan, at Geliloth by the Jordan
opposite the Israelite side. When the news reached them, 12
all the community of the Israelites assembled at Shiloh to
advance against them with a display of force. At the same 13
time the Israelites sent Phinehas son of Eleazar the priest
into the land of Gilead, to the Reubenites, the Gadites,
and the half tribe of Manasseh, and ten leading men[b] with 14
him, one from each of the tribes of Israel, each of them
the head of a household among the clans of Israel. They 15
came to the Reubenites, the Gadites, and the half tribe
of Manasseh in the land of Gilead, and remonstrated with
them in these words: 'We speak for the whole com- 16
munity of the LORD. What is this treachery you have
committed against the God of Israel? Are you ceasing to
follow the LORD and building your own altar this day in
defiance of the LORD? Remember our offence at Peor, for 17
which a plague fell upon the community of the LORD; to
this day we have not been purified from it. Was that
offence so slight that you dare cease to follow the LORD 18

[a] *Prob. rdg.; Heb. adds* which was in Canaan.
[b] *So Pesh.; Heb. adds* by households.

today? If you defy the LORD today, then tomorrow he
19 will be angry with the whole community of Israel. If the
land you have taken is unclean, then cross over to the
LORD's own land, where the Tabernacle of the LORD now
rests, and take a share of it with us; but do not defy the
LORD and involve us in your defiance by building an
altar of your own apart from the altar of the LORD our
20 God. Remember the treachery of Achan son of Zerah,
who defied the ban and the whole community of Israel
suffered for it. He was not the only one who paid for
that sin with his life.'

21   Then the Reubenites, the Gadites, and the half tribe of
Manasseh remonstrated with the heads of the clans of
22 Israel: 'The LORD the God of gods, the LORD the God of
gods, he knows, and Israel must know: if this had been
an act of defiance or treachery against the LORD, you
23 could not save us today. If we had built ourselves an
altar meaning to forsake the LORD, or had offered whole-
offerings and grain-offerings upon it, or had presented
shared-offerings, the LORD himself would exact punish-
24 ment. The truth is that we have done this for fear[a] that
the day may come when your sons will say to ours,
"What have you to do with the LORD, the God of Israel?
25 The LORD put the Jordan as a boundary between our sons
and your sons. You have no share in the LORD, you men
of Reuben and Gad." Thus your sons will prevent our
26 sons from going in awe of the LORD. So we resolved to
set ourselves to build an altar, not for whole-offerings
27 and sacrifices, but as a witness between us and you, and
between our descendants after us. Thus we shall be able

[a] *So Pesh.; Heb. adds* from a word.

to do service before the LORD, as we do now, with our whole-offerings, our sacrifices, and our shared-offerings; and your sons will never be able to say to our sons that they have no share in the LORD. And we thought, if ever 28 they do say this to us and our descendants, we will point to this copy of the altar of the LORD which we have made, not for whole-offerings and not for sacrifices, but as a witness between us and you. God forbid that we should 29 defy the LORD and forsake him this day by building another altar for whole-offerings, grain-offerings, and sacrifices, in addition to the altar of the LORD our God which stands in front of his Tabernacle.'

When Phinehas the priest and the leaders of the com- 30 munity, the heads of the Israelite clans, who were with him, heard what the Reubenites, the Gadites, and the Manassites said, they were satisfied. Phinehas son of 31 Eleazar the priest said to the Reubenites, Gadites, and Manassites, 'We know now that the LORD is in our midst today; you have not acted treacherously against the LORD, and thus you have preserved all Israel from punishment at his hand.' Then Phinehas son of Eleazar the 32 priest and the leaders left the Reubenites and the Gadites in Gilead and reported to the Israelites in Canaan. The 33 Israelites were satisfied, and they blessed God and thought no more of attacking Reuben and Gad and ravaging their land. The Reubenites and Gadites said, 'The altar is a 34 witness between us that the LORD is God', and they named it 'Witness'.[a]

⁎ At least on the surface these paragraphs tell a simple and direct story. As the Transjordanian tribes were returning to

[a] Witness: *so some MSS.; others om.*

their own land they built a 'great altar' near the Jordan, provoking the other tribes to threaten military action against them (verses 9–12). But the tribes were persuaded to withhold their attack while a delegation under the leadership of the priest Phinehas went to admonish the two-and-a-half tribes and to ask for an explanation of what appeared to be an act of treachery 'against the God of Israel' (verses 13–20). The Transjordanian tribes insisted that they had committed no sin, since they had not built the altar for sacrifices but as 'a witness', to remind their own descendants that they were part of Israel and that they too worship the LORD (verses 21–9). The delegation was satisfied, the altar allowed to stand, and peace maintained among the tribes (verses 30–4). It is noteworthy that the figure of Joshua does not appear in the story.

The language of the chapter is Deuteronomistic, and the editor's purpose in telling the story is transparent. As most commentators have recognized, the writer is interested in giving a warning against illegitimate cults and cult places. It is taken for granted that there can be only one proper place of worship. After the seventh century B.C., that one place would be Jerusalem, but the idea of a single sanctuary – probably wherever the Ark was located – was much more ancient.

And it seems clear that the writer did not invent the story but rather depended upon old traditions. Behind the present narrative stands at least the existence of the 'great altar' and some account of its establishment. The editor has explained that embarrassing fact and turned it to his advantage, making it the occasion for a sermon about apostasy. In the reform of Josiah, with which the book of Deuteronomy is associated, all sanctuaries outside of Jerusalem were ordered to be destroyed (cp. 2 Kings 22–3). One can only speculate about the shape and meaning of the story before it was so thoroughly revised. Some commentators have suggested that it originally was an aetiology for a holy place or its name. Others have argued that behind this story stands an ancient ceremony by which the tribes east and west of the Jordan were united. It is true that there are significant parallels between this story and the account of the establishment of a peaceful boundary between Jacob and Laban (Gen. 31: 43–54). In both cases a monument on the boundary was called 'witness' and peaceful relations followed.

The account stresses the unity of all twelve tribes of Israel, on both sides of the Jordan, but the perspective is betrayed when the western side is called 'the LORD's own land' (verse 19). In fact, other violent conflicts between the tribes on the east and west were known. Judg. 12: 1–6 reports that Jephthah, a 'judge over Israel' from the tribe of Manasseh in Transjordan, attacked the tribe of Ephraim in the west. Thus one can understand not only the Deuteronomistic historian's interest in stressing purity of worship but also his concern to emphasize the unity of all Israel.

9. It is assumed that Joshua and Israel are at *Shiloh* where they had gone for the final stages of the division of the land (18: 1; 19: 51; 21: 2). The city has been identified with Khirbet Seilūn in the central hill-country north of Ai (see Map 1 and the Gazetteer). The place was an important cultic centre which was the home of the Ark during some periods (cp. 1 Sam. 1–4).

10. It is difficult to determine whether the *great altar* was east or west of the Jordan. The Hebrew of this verse (see N.E.B. footnote) has it on the west while the next verse places it on the other side. Instead of *Geliloth* Codex Vaticanus, a fourth-century A.D. manuscript of the Septuagint, reads 'Gilgal'. The report of the altar in this area recalls the story of the crossing of the Jordan and the memorial stones (chs. 3–4), as well as the reference to 'the Carved Stones' at Gilgal in Judg. 3: 19, 26.

13. *Phinehas son of Eleazar* appears in Num. 25: 6–18 as the one who stemmed a plague by vigorously opposing apostasy. The name 'Phinehas' also appears in connection with the sanctuary at Shiloh as one of the sons of Eli (1 Sam. 1: 3; 4: 4).

Phinehas is very important in later tradition (cp. Ps. 106: 30); Ecclus. 45: 23 lists him as 'third in renown'.

14. *ten leading men*: that is, one from each of the nine-and-a-half tribes west of the Jordan.

17. *at Peor*: an allusion to the apostasy stopped by Phinehas (Num. 25: 6–18).

18. The idea of corporate guilt is taken for granted (see comments on 7: 1).

19. *Tabernacle of the LORD*: perhaps intended as a reference to the 'Tent of the Presence', reportedly established at Shiloh (18: 1, see comments). The term occurs most commonly in the Priestly document (see *The Making of the Old Testament*, pp. 60ff., in this series on literary sources) in reference to the central place of worship.

23. This *altar* will not serve the function of a true altar, thus it cannot be a rival to the central sanctuary.

34. '*Witness*': the language suggests the establishment of peaceful relations between tribes (cp. Gen. 31: 43–54). ✳

Joshua's farewell and death

JOSHUA'S FIRST FAREWELL ADDRESS

23 A LONG TIME HAD PASSED since the LORD had given Israel security from all the enemies who surrounded 2 them, and Joshua was now a very old man. He summoned all Israel, their elders and heads of families, their judges and officers, and said to them, 'I have become a very old 3 man. You have seen for yourselves all that the LORD our God has done to these peoples for your sake; it was the 4 LORD God himself who fought for you. I have allotted you your patrimony tribe by tribe, the land of all the peoples that I have wiped out and of all these that remain

between the Jordan and the Great Sea which lies towards
the setting sun. The LORD your God himself drove them 5
out for your sake; he drove them out to make room for
you, and you occupied their land, as the LORD your God
had promised you. Be resolute therefore: observe and 6
perform everything written in the book of the law of
Moses, without swerving to right or to left. You must 7
not associate with the peoples that are left among you;
you must not call upon their gods by name, nor*a* swear
by them nor prostrate yourselves in worship before them.
You must hold fast to the LORD your God as you have 8
done down to this day. For your sake the LORD has driven 9
out great and mighty nations; to this day not a man of
them has withstood you. One of you can put to flight a 10
thousand, because the LORD your God fights for you, as
he promised. Be on your guard then, love the LORD your 11
God, for*b* if you do turn away and attach yourselves to 12
the peoples that still remain among you, and intermarry
with them and associate with them and they with you,
then be sure that the LORD will not continue to drive 13
those peoples out to make room for you. They will be
snares to entrap you, whips for your backs and barbed
hooks in your eyes, until you vanish from the good land
which the LORD your God has given you. And now I 14
am going the way of all mankind. You know in your
heart of hearts that nothing that the LORD your God has
promised you has failed to come true, every word of it.
But the same LORD God who has kept his word to you 15

[*a*] you must not call...nor: *or* the name of their gods shall not be your
boast, nor must you...
[*b*] Be on...for: *or* Take very good care to love the LORD your God,
but...

173

to such good effect can equally bring every kind of evil
on you, until he has rooted you out from this good land
16 which he has given you. If you break the covenant which
the LORD your God has prescribed and prostrate yourselves in worship before other gods, then the LORD will
be angry with you and you will quickly vanish from the
good land he has given you.'

✻ This passage is a single, complete unit with a clear introduction and a logical conclusion. The next section begins
with a new introduction (24: 1). Nevertheless, the settings of
both ch. 23 and 24: 1-28 are established by the same fact,
the report of the death and burial of Joshua in 24: 29-31.
These sections present the last testamentary activities of Joshua.
Both have the appearance of the last will and testament of
Israel's great leader. Such final activities – including speeches
and pronouncement of blessings – were well known in the
ancient Near East. The Old Testament reports the final words
of Jacob (Gen. 48-9), including his blessings for each of his
sons, and the last instructions of David to his son Solomon
(1 Kings 2: 1-9; cp. 2 Sam. 23: 1-7). Most of the book of
Deuteronomy is presented as the last testament of Moses (see
especially Deut. 32-3). Thus the section gives a final parallel
between the lives of Moses and Joshua.

This unit in its entirety is the work of the Deuteronomistic
historian, who has polished the tradition of the last testaments
into literary convention. (The fact that 24: 1 parallels 23: 1
suggests the possibility that the book was edited more than
once under the influence of the tradition of Deuteronomy.)
Following the introduction (verses 1-2a), both style and
content characterize the address as a sermon (see comments
on ch. 1, pp. 21ff.). Joshua addresses Israel directly in the second
person ('You have seen', 'I have allotted you', 'you must',
'you must not'), and tries to place his words on the hearts of
his listeners. He speaks unambiguously but repetitiously.

Three motifs run through the sermon. First, there are re-
minders of what the LORD has done for Israel (verses 3–5,
9–10, 14). Second, there are admonitions to obey the law
(verses 6–8, 11). Third, there are warnings that the LORD will
punish Israel if she is disobedient (verses 12–13, 15–16). Some
of the admonitions to obey are quite general, but others are
very specific. In both the specific admonitions (verse 7) and
the warnings the Deuteronomistic historian focuses upon
what was for him the single most fearful problem, apostasy.
He was gravely concerned that Israel should not worship any
gods but the LORD, nor even acknowledge their existence by
so much as mentioning their names, nor participate in any
activity – such as association or intermarriage with pagans –
which could lead to false worship. The writer reveals the
situation in which he is writing, the Babylonian exile. When
he has Joshua threaten that if Israel is disobedient she will
'vanish from the good land' which the LORD has given (verses
13, 15, 16), he is writing to and for the people who have in fact
been uprooted from Palestine to Babylon. Thus he advances
his explanation of the exile as the judgement of God upon his
disobedient people and encourages them to avoid the mistakes
of the past.

1. *security*: see comments on 1: 13, 15.

2. In contrast to 24: 1, which specifies that Joshua called
the tribes to Shechem, the place of this assembly is not given.
The previous chapter (22: 9) suggests Shiloh as the location.

4. *the Great Sea*: the Mediterranean. Again, the editor
describes all of the territory west of the Jordan as both conquered and settled, while the individual stories and lists had
included less.

6. *the book of the law of Moses*: see comments on 1: 8.

7. Any activity which would imply the existence of the
gods of the foreigners is prohibited. Such a rigorous command
could have been occasioned only by strong temptations.

11. The command to *love the LORD your God* is character-
istic of the book of Deuteronomy, where it is based upon the

LORD's own love for his people: 'it was because the LORD loved you and stood by his oath to your forefathers, that he brought you out with his strong hand and redeemed you from the land of slavery' (Deut. 7: 8; cp. also Deut. 11: 1).

12. For the Deuteronomistic historian, intermarriage was dangerous because of the possibility that it could lead to the worship of pagan gods.

13. *continue to drive those peoples out*: it is assumed – contrary to verse 4 – that the conquest is not complete but must be a continuing activity. This point will be explained more fully in Judg. 2: 16 – 3: 6.

14. The N.E.B. translates the Septuagint. The Hebrew reads literally, 'Behold, *today* I am going the way of all the earth.'

16. The reference to *the covenant* is a link with the report of the covenant ceremony in the next chapter. The term *covenant* refers here specifically to the stipulations in the agreement to which Israel has sworn, that is, the laws. ✴

JOSHUA'S SECOND FAREWELL ADDRESS
AND THE COVENANT AT SHECHEM

24 Joshua assembled all the tribes of Israel at Shechem. He summoned the elders of Israel, the heads of families, the judges and officers; and they presented themselves 2 before God. Joshua then said this to all the people: 'This is the word of the LORD the God of Israel: "Long ago your forefathers, Terah and his sons Abraham and Nahor, lived beside the Euphrates, and they worshipped other 3 gods. I took your father Abraham from beside the Euphrates and led him through the length and breadth of Canaan. I gave him many descendants: I gave him Isaac, 4 and to Isaac I gave Jacob and Esau. I put Esau in possession of the hill-country of Seir, but Jacob and his sons went

down to Egypt. I sent Moses and Aaron, and I struck the 5
Egyptians with plagues – you know well what I did
among them – and after that I brought you out; I brought 6
your fathers out of Egypt and you came to the Red Sea.
The Egyptians sent their chariots and cavalry to pursue
your fathers to the sea. But when they appealed to the 7
LORD, he put a screen of darkness between you and the
Egyptians, and brought the sea down on them and it
covered them; you saw for yourselves what I did to
Egypt. For a long time you lived in the wilderness. Then 8
I brought you into the land of the Amorites who lived
east of the Jordan; they fought against you, but I delivered
them into your hands; you took possession of their
country and I destroyed them for your sake. The king of 9
Moab, Balak son of Zippor, took the field against Israel.
He sent for Balaam son of Beor to lay a curse on you, but 10
I would not listen to him. Instead of that he blessed you;
and so I saved you from the power of Balak. Then you 11
crossed the Jordan and came to Jericho. The citizens of
Jericho fought against you,[a] but I delivered them into
your hands. I spread panic before you, and it was this, 12
not your sword or your bow, that drove out the two
kings of the Amorites. I gave you land on which you 13
had not laboured, cities which you had never built; you
have lived in those cities and you eat the produce of
vineyards and olive-groves which you did not plant."

'Hold the LORD in awe then, and worship him in 14
loyalty and truth. Banish the gods whom your fathers
worshipped beside the Euphrates and in Egypt, and

[a] *Prob. rdg.; Heb. adds* Amorites, Perizzites, Canaanites, Hittites,
Girgashites, Hivites, and Jebusites.

15 worship the LORD. But if it does not please you to worship the LORD, choose here and now whom you will worship: the gods whom your forefathers worshipped beside the Euphrates, or the gods of the Amorites in whose land you are living. But I and my family, we will worship the

16 LORD.' The people answered, 'God forbid that we should

17 forsake the LORD to worship other gods, for it was the LORD our God who brought us and our fathers up from Egypt, that land of slavery; it was he who displayed those great signs before our eyes and guarded us on all our wanderings among the many peoples through whose

18 lands we passed. The LORD drove out before us the Amorites and all the peoples who lived in that country.

19 We too will worship the LORD; he is our God.' Joshua answered the people, 'You cannot worship the LORD. He is a holy god, a jealous god, and he will not forgive

20 your rebellion and your sins. If you forsake the LORD and worship foreign gods, he will turn and bring adversity upon you and, although he once brought you pros-

21 perity, he will make an end of you.' The people said to

22 Joshua, 'No; we will worship the LORD.' He said to them, 'You are witnesses against yourselves that you have chosen the LORD and will worship him.' 'Yes,' they

23 answered, 'we are witnesses.' He said to them, 'Then here and now banish the foreign gods that are among you,

24 and turn your hearts to the LORD the God of Israel.' The people said to Joshua, 'The LORD our God we will

25 worship and his voice we will obey.' So Joshua made a covenant that day with*a* the people; he drew up a statute

26 and an ordinance for them in Shechem and wrote its

[*a*] *Or* for.

178

terms in the book of the law of God. He took a great
stone and set it up there under the terebinth[a] in the
sanctuary of the LORD, and said to all the people, 'This 27
stone is a witness against us; for it has heard all the words
which the LORD has spoken to us. If you renounce your
God, it shall be a witness against you.' Then Joshua dis- 28
missed the people, each man to his patrimony.

✶ The report of Joshua's final words and deeds stands out in
the book, not only because of its significance but also because
of its relationship to the context. Because it repeats some of
the previous unit – both purport to give Joshua's last words,
but apparently at different locations – the section seems to be
a later appendix to the book of Joshua. Furthermore, there are
very few connections with the earlier record. The reference
to the fight with the citizens of Jericho (verse 11)contradicts
ch. 6, and in contrast to the remainder of the book verses 15
and 18 speak of all the population of west Jordan as Amorites.
The dating of these events at the end of Joshua's lifetime is
given only by the context, not by the report itself. The story
does not deal specifically with the last will and testament of
Joshua; it only follows the pattern of some of the last words
and deeds of Moses as reported in the book of Deuteronomy.

While the account has been reworked thoroughly by an
editor in the school of Deuteronomy, it is based upon very
old oral or written traditions. The presence of multiple
traditions is seen, for example, in the inconsistent changes of
speaker: the LORD himself is speaking (through Joshua) in
verses 2*b*–13 but in verse 7 he refers to himself in the third
person. More revealing is the fact that the basic narrative
reflects ideas and institutions of Israel's earliest tribal league.

The report can be understood more fully when it is outlined
in the following manner: (1) Introduction (verses 1–2*a*). The
people are summoned to Shechem to hear Joshua. (2) Joshua's

[a] *Or* pole.

speech, presenting 'the word of the LORD' (verses 2a–13). The history of the LORD's actions on behalf of his people is recited as the basis for faith. (3) Joshua's challenge and the positive response of the people (verses 14–24). The issue is posed more than once but each time Israel affirms her faith. (4) Covenant ceremonies (verses 25–7). The terms of the covenant are recorded and a monument is established. (5) Dismissal of the people (verse 28).

It is apparent that an event of high religious significance is being described. Each facet of the report reflects liturgical practices. The people are summoned formally to appear before God (verse 1); Joshua's account of the history of Israel parallels other recitals (Exod. 19ff.; Deut. 6: 20–5; 26: 5–10) which have been related to covenant ceremonies; the antiphonal responses to Joshua's challenges are formal pledges; and the final events (verses 25–7) are characterized explicitly as establishing a covenant. Furthermore, scholars have noted the parallels between these events and ancient Near Eastern treaties – covenants among nations. In short, the unit describes an ancient Israelite covenant ceremony. While it is possible that the report remembers some specific covenant ceremony – such as the unification of Israelite tribal groups or the initiation of the inhabitants of the region of Shechem into Israel – it is much more likely that the unit is based upon the institution of the regular renewal of the covenant between the tribes and the LORD during the period of the judges. On such occasions the tribes would have assembled to reaffirm their allegiance to the LORD and thus their relationship to one another. It is not known how often such ceremonies were held.

The focal point of the report is Joshua's initial challenge and the people's first response (verses 14–18). The basic question is whether Israel will serve the LORD or other gods. That choice is the central concern in the book of Deuteronomy, but it was also the main element in the covenant itself, in which Israel became the LORD's people and he became their God. The laws (cp. verse 26) spelled out what it meant to be

faithful to the LORD. It is possible that deep in the background
of this affirmation of allegiance to the LORD lies a ceremony in
which all other deities were renounced formally. Gen. 35: 2–4
seems to report such a ceremony at Shechem.

In its final form and location within the Deuteronomistic
history of Israel (see pp. 14–17), the purpose of this report is
entirely positive. The book was not allowed to conclude on a
negative note (23: 15–16). While the writer seems to allude
to the 'adversity' of the Babylonian exile (verses 19–20), by
reporting the renewal of the covenant he wants to make it clear
that the covenant can be renewed once again if Israel is willing
to respond positively – as her ancestors did in the time of Joshua.

1. *Shechem*: on the identification and location of the site,
see comment on 8: 30, Map 1 and the Gazetteer. The Septuagint reads 'Shiloh' at this point and in verse 25. That the
people presented themselves before God indicates the presence
of a sanctuary. In 8: 30–5 the building of an altar in the area
is reported, but Shechem was remembered as one of Israel's
most ancient sacred places. According to Gen. 12: 6–7,
Abraham established an altar there. The recent archaeological
excavations of the site have uncovered a sacred precinct which
was used about 1800–1100 B.C.

2. *This is the word of the LORD*: literally, 'thus says (or
said) the LORD'. Joshua's address begins with the messenger
formula typically used by prophets to indicate that the words
which follow are not their own but God's (see, e.g., Amos
1: 3, 6, 9 etc.).

The recital of Israel's history which begins here is not derived
directly from any particular pentateuchal source, but rather
is a literary elaboration of the confession of Israel's faith in
historical terms (cp. Deut. 6: 20–5). The book of Genesis is
seldom specific about the *other gods* worshipped by the patriarchs; the reference at this point lays the foundation for the
rejection of those deities later (verses 15–20).

3. *many descendants*: an allusion to the fulfilment of the
promise reported in Gen. 12: 1–3; 15: 4–5 and elsewhere.

5. The verse presents textual problems. *I sent Moses and Aaron* is missing in the Septuagint. Instead of *and I struck... what I did among them*, read perhaps with Codex Alexandrinus, a fourth-century A.D. manuscript of the Septuagint: 'and I plagued Egypt with the signs which I did among them'.

6. *the Red Sea*: Hebrew, 'Sea of Reeds'. See Exod. 14.

8-9. See Num. 21 and Deut. 2-3 for the defeat of the Amorites, and Num. 22-4 and Deut. 23: 4-5 for the story of Balaam.

11. As noted above, this version of the capture of Jericho is not consistent with ch. 6, which reports no fight.

12. *two kings*: the Septuagint reads 'twelve kings'. Both the Hebrew and the Septuagint disagree with the remainder of the book; 12: 7-24 lists 'thirty-one kings in all'.

14. *the gods*: the motif of verse 2 is resumed, with the additional reference to *Egypt*. It is taken for granted that Israel's ancestors worshipped pagan deities until the time of Moses.

17-18. The central elements of the recital in verses 2-13 – the exodus, the preservation in the wilderness and the granting of the promised land – are repeated as the foundation for the people's faith.

19-20. The implications of commitment to the LORD are made clear. Since he is a *holy god* he cannot be worshipped alongside others but demands total allegiance. *jealous god*: cp. Exod. 20:5; 34:14; Deut. 5: 9.

21-2. *You are witnesses...we are witnesses*: the formulas derive from the procedures of civil law; through these expressions contracts were attested (cp. Ruth 4: 9-11).

23-4. See Gen. 35: 2-4 for a similar renunciation of other gods.

26. *the book of the law of God*: see comments on 1: 8. The writing of the law is similar to the report in 8: 30-5. The *terebinth* at Shechem is mentioned in Gen. 12: 6.

27. The exact function of the 'great stone' is obscure. It is possible that the terms of the agreement were inscribed on it,

but that is not stated. The use of standing stones such as this one were strongly prohibited in the book of Deuteronomy (16: 22). Remnants of the old idea of such stones as monuments to covenantal agreements are probably seen in the report of the pact between Jacob and Laban (Gen. 31: 43–54; see also Gen. 28: 18 and the comments on Josh. 22: 9–34). ✳

THE TOMBS OF JOSHUA, JOSEPH AND ELEAZAR

After these things, Joshua son of Nun the servant of the 29 LORD died; he was a hundred and ten years old. They 30 buried him within the border of his own patrimony in Timnath-serah in the hill-country of Ephraim to the north of Mount Gaash. Israel served the LORD during the 31 lifetime of Joshua and of the elders who outlived him and who well knew all that the LORD had done for Israel.

The bones of Joseph, which the Israelites had brought 32 up from Egypt, were buried in Shechem, in the plot of land which Jacob had bought from the sons of Hamor father of Shechem for a hundred sheep;[a] and they passed into the patrimony of the house of Joseph. Eleazar son 33 of Aaron died and was buried in the hill which had been given to Phinehas his son in the hill-country of Ephraim.

✳ Three burial traditions conclude the book. Two factors link the traditions concerning Joshua and Eleazar: they belonged to the same generation and they were buried in the same region, 'the hill-country of Ephraim'. The report of the interment of the bones of Joseph concludes a motif which had been maintained since Gen. 50: 25 (see also Exod. 13: 19). When Joseph died in Egypt he made his family vow that they would not leave his body in the foreign land.

[a] *Or* pieces of money (*cp. Gen. 33: 19; Job 42: 11*).

29–31. This report is repeated in Judg. 2: 7–9. In 19: 49–51 (see comments) it is noted that Joshua was given a special allotment within the lands of his tribe of Ephraim in *Timnath-serah* (Judg. 2: 9 gives the name as 'Timnath-heres'). The editor does not glorify Joshua as he did Moses (Deut. 34:5–12); it was sufficient for him to note that during his leadership *Israel served the LORD.*

32. The purchase of the land now used for the burial of Joseph was noted in Gen. 33: 18–20. Shechem was located within the territory of the Joseph tribes (17: 7).

33. The reference to *the hill which had been given to Phinehas* probably contains the proper name of the place, 'Gibeath-Phinehas'. ✳

✳   ✳   ✳   ✳   ✳   ✳   ✳   ✳   ✳   ✳   ✳   ✳   ✳

A NOTE ON FURTHER READING

A good detailed commentary is J. Alberto Soggin, *Joshua* (S.C.M. and Westminster, Old Testament Library, translated in 1972). The present study makes substantial use of the work of the German scholar, Martin Noth, whose commentary (1953) is a standard work, paying particular attention to the problems of the literary and pre-literary history of the book. John Bright's commentary in *The Interpreter's Bible* (Abingdon Press, 1953) and John Gray, *Joshua, Judges and Ruth* (New Century Bible, Nelsons, now Oliphants, 1967), may also be usefully consulted. Background information concerning any name or topic mentioned in the Bible may be found in *The Interpreter's Dictionary of the Bible* (Abingdon Press, 1962).

For the history of Israel, see especially Martin Noth, *The History of Israel* (A. and C. Black; Harper and Row, revised translation 1960) and John Bright, *A History of Israel* (S.C.M. Old Testament Library and Westminster Press, revised ed. 1972).

For geographical and archaeological matters, see Denis Baly, *Geographical Companion to the Bible* (McGraw-Hill, 1963) and Y. Aharoni, *The Land of the Bible* (Westminster Press, translated in 1967). A good biblical atlas, such as the *Oxford Bible Atlas*, ed. by H. G. May (Oxford University Press, 1962), should also be consulted.

GEOGRAPHICAL TERMS IN JOSHUA

Arnon, 'the gorge of the Arnon' Called today the Wadi el-Mūjib. Josh. 12: 1–2; 13: 9, 16. The Arnon river descends 1070 metres (3500 feet) through a steep-sided, narrow and deep gorge, 48 kilometres (30 miles) long, and flows into the Dead Sea at approximately the middle of its eastern shore. The Arnon marked the southern limit of Israel's territorial claims in the Transjordan.

Arabah Generally any part of the geological rift which extends from the Sea of Kinnereth (Galilee) down the course of the Jordan River to 'the Sea of the Arabah' (the Dead Sea) and beyond to the Gulf of Aqabah. 'The Arabah opposite Kinnereth' and 'the eastern Arabah' refer to that portion of the rift east of Kinnereth and the Jordan respectively. 'The Arabah' is sometimes used in the Old Testament to refer more specifically to that portion of the rift below the Dead Sea.

'The bare mountain which leads up to Seir' (or 'Mount Halak which leads up to Seir') Probably to be identified with Jebel Ḥalāq, north-by-north-east of 'Abdeh. According to Josh. 11: 17 and 12: 7, this mountain marked the southern limits of Israel's territorial claims west of the Jordan.

Bashan The rich pasture-land east of the Sea of Kinnereth and the sources of the Jordan. Included the Yarmuk and territory northward as far as Mount Hermon and eastward as far as Salcah. Josh. 9: 10; 12: 4–5; 13: 1–12; etc.

'The desert' (Hebrew *hammidbār*) The biblical writers use this term to refer variously to the barren areas of Sinai, the lower Negeb, and the southern and eastern Transjordan. The same term is occasionally translated 'wilderness' in N.E.B. (e.g. Josh. 5: 4–6).

Galilee The mountainous area between the Sea of Galilee (Kinnereth) and the Great Sea (the Mediterranean). Josh. 20: 7; 21: 32.

Gilead The mountainous area east of the Jordan, bisected by the Jabbok. Josh. 12: 2, 5; 13: 11, 25, 31; 17: 1, etc.

Jabbok, 'the gorge of the Jabbok' Called today the Nahr ez-Zerqā. A large tributary of the Jordan which drops 975 metres (3200 feet) as it cuts through the mountainous region of Gilead. It is said to have marked the northern limits of Sihon's kingdom. (Josh. 12: 2).

Jarkon (present-day Nahal Yarqon) A river which rises at the site of ancient Aphek (near present-day Rosh Ha'Ayin) and empties into the Mediterranean Sea near the modern city of Tel Aviv. Appears only in Josh. 19: 46, which is itself textually problematic.

Jordan   The river which reaches from the foot of Mount Hermon to the northern end of the Dead Sea, and the valley which it occupies.

Kanah, 'the gorge of Kanah'   Called today the Wadi Qānah. The sources of this wadi lie south-west of the site of ancient Shechem (near present-day Nablus) in the western watershed of the central hill-country. It joins the Jarkon (Nahal Yarqon) not far from the latter's source.

Sea of Kinnereth   Also called the 'Sea of Galilee'. The name is probably derived from Kinnereth, a city of Naphtali (Josh. 19: 35), which was probably situated on its shore. This lake, which is about 18 metres (600 feet) below sea level, is approximately 19 kilometres long by 8 kilometres wide (12 miles by 5 miles). Josh. 11: 2; 12: 3; 13: 27.

The Lebanon   Generally, the mountainous area north of Palestine, including both the Lebanon and Anti-Lebanon mountain ranges.

Misrephoth on the west (literally, 'Misrephoth-maim')   Appears only in Josh. 11: 8 and 13: 6, where it is associated with 'Greater Sidon'. It is unclear whether Misrephoth-maim refers to a particular site or to a locality.

Mount Carmel   The north-western spur of the central hill-country which extends to, and juts out into, the Mediterranean Sea immediately south of Haifa.

Mount Ebal   Mounts Ebal and Gerizim are two prominent heights which overlook the pass through the central hill-country at Shechem. Mount Ebal was situated on the north, Gerizim on the south, and the city of Shechem in between. Josh. 8: 30, 33.

Mount Gaash   An unidentified mountain in the Ephraimite portion of the central hill-country. Reported in Josh. 24: 30 and Judg. 2: 9 to be situated immediately north of Joshua's grave.

Mount Gerizim: See Mount Ebal.

Mount Heres   An unidentified mountain in the territory allotted to Dan. Judg. 1: 35 (cp. Josh. 19: 41ff.).

Mount Hermon   The tallest (about 2740 metres or 9000 feet) and southernmost spur of the Anti-Lebanon range. Josh. 11: 3, 17; 12: 1, 5; 13: 5, 11.

Mount Tabor   A solitary hill (about 510 metres or 1700 feet) in the 'Vale of Jezreel'. Was apparently bounded by Zebulun, Issachar, and Naphtali. Josh. 19: 22, 34.

Negeb   The 'dry land' area south of Beersheba and extending from the Gulf of Aqabah to Gaza. This area is mountainous in the central and southern parts with deep wadis.

Pisgah, 'watershed of Pisgah'   Either a section of the mountains of Abarim which overlook the north-eastern shores of the Dead Sea, or a particular promontory of that range. Moses is said to have viewed the promised land from Pisgah (Deut. 3: 27); and Sihon's kingdom is said to have extended as far as the eastern side of the Sea of Arabah below 'the watershed of Pisgah' (Josh. 12: 3).

Seir   The name means 'Hairy' or 'Shaggy', and is generally associated in the Old Testament with Edom (e.g. Josh. 24: 4). Josh. 11: 17 and 12: 7 place this Edomite Seir (or possibly another Seir) west of the Arabah, however, and Josh. 15: 10 knows of a Mount Seir along Judah's north-western boundary.

Shephelah   The 'foothills' which lie between the coastal (Philistine) plain and the hill-country of Judah.

Torrent of Egypt   The Wadi el-'Arīsh which enters the Mediterranean Sea at el'Arīsh.

Vale of Achor   A valley which was located near Jericho (Josh. 7: 24, 26) and Judah's north-eastern boundary (Josh. 15: 7). Probably to be identified with the present-day el-Buqei'ah.

Vale of Aijalon   A valley north-west of Jerusalem which provides an entrance into the hill-country from the Shephelah. It was in connection with a battle fought in this vicinity that the sun is said to have stood still (Josh. 10: 12–13). See 'Aijalon' in the Gazetteer.

Vale of Jezreel   Josh. 17: 16. The valley which separates Galilee from Mount Carmel and the central hill-country. The name can be used to refer more specifically to that portion of the valley in the immediate vicinity of the village Jezreel (see Gazetteer).

Vale of Mizpah   The precise location is uncertain, although Josh. 11: 8 clearly places it near the northern limits of Israel's territorial claims, apparently near the foot of Mount Hermon.

Vale of Rephaim   A valley near the Judah–Benjamin tribal boundary (Josh. 15: 8; 18: 16). It is generally believed, on the basis of the boundary description, to have been situated south-west of Jerusalem. This evidence is problematic, however, and 2 Sam. 5: 22–5 (paralleled by 1 Chron. 14: 13–17) would seem to place the Vale of Rephaim further to the north.

'The waters of Merom'   Josh. 11: 5, 7. Often associated with the Wadi Meirūn which flows into the Sea of Galilee. But see commentary on Josh. 11: 5. See also the entry under 'Shimron' in the Gazetteer.

Zin, 'the wilderness of Zin'   Josh. 15: 1–3. A portion of the wilderness (see entry under 'desert') near Judah's southern border. The Israelites are said to have passed through the wilderness of Zin on their journey to Canaan from Egypt (Num. 13: 21; 20: 1; 27: 14, etc.).

GAZETTEER

The location of the ancient cities and villages which appear in the biblical texts cannot always be established with certainty. Three kinds of evidence must be taken into consideration in each case: (1) The contexts in which a city is mentioned in the ancient writings will sometimes indicate the general vicinity in which it was located, and occasionally provide information about the surrounding topography. It is apparent from the narrative in 4: 15–20, for example, that Gilgal and Jericho were situated in the lower Jordan valley and near each other. (2) The name of an ancient city will often suggest its topographical character. Moreover, the ancient names have sometimes been preserved through the ages so that they are still recognizable in the present-day Arab names. Thus the name of biblical Geba (which means 'hill') is preserved in that of the present-day village of Jeba', which is located on a prominent hill north of Jerusalem. Caution is necessary, however, in that the name is not always preserved at the exact location of the ancient site. This is especially true with regard to the modern Israeli settlements which occasionally revive the name of a biblical city thought to have been located in the vicinity. (3) Finally, archaeological evidence is often helpful in establishing the location of an ancient city, although archaeological evidence is rarely conclusive in itself. The maps in this volume and the Gazetteer below include the names of the cities which appear in Joshua and whose general vicinity can be established with some degree of certainty. When the city can be associated more specifically with an archaeological site, or with a present-day village which appears to have preserved the ancient name, the present-day name is indicated.

Abdon   (Khirbet 'Abdeh). 21: 30. Probably the same as Ebron in 19: 28 (footnote). Maps 5, 6.

Acco   (Tell el-Fukhkhār). 19: 30 (probable reading). Map 5.

Achzib   (ez-Zīb). 19: 29. To be distinguished from the Achzib which appears in the Judaean city list (15: 44). Map 5.

Adam   Appears only in 3: 16, where it is described as 'a town near Zarethan'. Scholars have generally associated Adam with Tell ed-Dāmiyeh, although 1 Kings 4: 12 would seem to place Zarethan much further to the north – i.e. in the vicinity of Beth-shean. 1 Kings 4: 12 reads, literally: 'and all Beth-shean which is beside Zarethan'. Map 1.

Adami-nekeb   (Khirbet Dāmiyeh). 19: 33. Map 5.

Adullam (esh-Sheikh Madhkūr). 12: 15; 15: 35. Maps 2, 3. The ancient name is preserved in that of Khirbet 'Id el-Mīyeh immediately to the north.

Ai (Khirbet et-Tell). 7: 1ff.; 12: 9. Maps 1, 2, 4.

Aijalon (Yālō). 19: 42; 21: 24. Maps 1, 4, 6. See also the reference to the 'Vale of Aijalon' in 10: 12.

Ain See Ashan.

Akshaph 19: 25 places Akshaph within Asher's territorial allotment, and the Egyptian records seem to place it more specifically in the area south-east of Acco. Tell Keisān and Khirbet el-Harbaj have both been proposed. Yet 11: 1 and 12: 20 seem to associate Akshaph with Madon and Shimron, which would suggest Khirbet Iksāf, about 14 kms (8 miles) east of Meirun. Possibly there was more than one city by this name. Maps 1, 2, 5.

Almon (Khirbet 'Almīt). 21: 18. Map 6.

Anab (Khirbet 'Anāb el-Kebīreh). 11: 21; 15: 50. Map 3.

Anaharath (possibly Tell el-Mukharkhash). 19: 19. Map 5.

Anathoth (Rās el-Kharrūbeh near 'Anātā). 21: 18. Map 6.

Anim (Khirbet Ghuwein et-Tahtā). 15: 50. Map 3.

Aphek Four different Apheks appear in the biblical records, three of them in the book of Joshua. (1) an Aphek on the Amorite frontier (13: 4; possibly Afqā, about 25 kms (15 miles) east of Jebeil; Map 1); (2) an Aphek in Asher's territorial allotment (19: 30; possibly Tell Kurdāneh; Map 5). (3) Aphek-in-Sharon (12: 18, according to the Septuagint; probably Rās el-'Ain or nearby Tell el-Muhmar; Map 2). The Aphek mentioned in 1 Kings 20: 26–30 and 2 Kings 13: 14–19 is generally associated with the present-day village of Fiq in Bashan. But a location in the Ephraimite hill-country would seem more likely; and the name may be preserved in that of Faqqū'a on Mount Gilboa (also called Jebel Faqqū'a).

Arab (Khirbet er-Rabīyeh). 15: 52. Map 3

Arad (Tell 'Arād). 12: 14. Maps 2, 3. Read. 'Arad' for 'Eder', in 15: 21.

Ararah (Khirbet 'Ar'arah). 15: 22. Map 3.

Aroer ('Arā'ir). 12: 2; 13: 9, 16. Located on the northern edge of the Arnon, near the crossing of the king's highway. Map 2. There was apparently another village with the same name located just west of Rabbah (13: 25).

Ashan (Khirbet 'Asan, approximately 2 kms (1 mile) north of Beer-sheba). 15: 42; 19: 7. Map 6. Read 'Ashan' instead of 'Ain' in 21: 16.

Ashdod (Esdūd). One of five Philistine cities listed in 13: 3. See also 11: 22; 15: 46–7. The other four were Gath (possibly Tell eṣ-Ṣāfi), Gaza (el-Ghazzeh), Ashkelon ('Asqalān), and Ekron (Khirbet el-Muqanna'). Map 1.

Ashkelon ('Asqalān). One of five Philistine cities mentioned in 13: 3. See 'Ashdod' above for the names and probable locations of the other four. Map 1.

Ashtaroth (Tell 'Ashtarah). 9: 10; 12: 4; 13: 12, 31. Maps 2, 6. Be-eshtarah in 21: 27 is probably a corrupt reading of Ashtaroth (cp. 1 Chron. 6: 71).

Ataroth, Ataroth-addar 16: 3, 5, 7; 18: 13. The name seems to be preserved in that of the present-day village, 'Aṭṭāra, located just south of Rāmallah at the foot of Tell en-Naṣbeh. But this village probably is not at the exact site of ancient Ataroth. Most scholars, in fact, identify Tell en-Naṣbeh as ancient Mizpah. Nor does it seem possible that the Ataroth in 16: 7 is identical with the one in 16: 3, 5 and 18: 13, since this would render the Ataroth–Naarath–Jericho–Jordan segment of Ephraim's boundary meaningless (see comment on 16: 6–7). Unless the text is corrupt, this reference in 16: 7 must be to another Ataroth between Janoah (Khirbet Yānūn) and Naarath (possibly Khirbet el-'Ayāsh). Map 4.

Azekah (Tell Zakarīyeh). 10: 10–11; 15: 35. Map 3.

Baal-gad Exact location uncertain, but it was apparently located near the base of Mount Hermon. 11: 17; 12: 7; 13: 5. Map 1.

Baither (Khirbet el-Yehūd near Bittīr). 15: 59 (Septuagint). Map 3.

Beeroth One of the four cities of the Gibeonite league (9: 18); also appears in the Judaean city list (18: 25). Has been associated variously with el-Bīreh (on the eastern outskirts of present-day Rāmallah), Tell en-Naṣbeh (approximately 3 kms (2 miles) south of Rāmallah), Nebi-Samwil (9 kms (5–6 miles) north-by-north-west of Jerusalem), and Khirbet el-Burj (slightly further south). Somewhere in the vicinity of the latter two seems more likely. Eusebius in the fourth century places Beeroth approximately this distance from Jerusalem; and the ancient name is probably preserved in that of Khirbet el-Biyar. Maps 1, 4.

Beersheba (Tell es-Seba' on the Wadi es-Seba'). 15: 28; 19: 2. Map 3.

Be-eshterah See Ashtaroth.

Bene-berak (Ibn Ibrāq near Tel Aviv). 19: 45. Map 4.

Beten The name is possibly preserved in that of Khirbet Ibīn, although Khirbet Ibṭīn seems to be situated more within the realm of Zebulun. 19: 25. Map 5.

Beth-anoth (Khirbet Beit'Anun). 15: 59. Map 3.

Beth-arabah ('Ain el-Gharabeh). 15: 6, 61; 18: 22. Maps 3, 4.

Beth-aven See Bethel.

Bethel (Beitīn). 7: 2; 8: 9, 12, 17; 12: 9, 16; 16: 1, 2; 18: 13, 22. Maps 1, 2, 3, 4. The connection between Bethel and Luz is unclear.

The two are equated in 18: 13, but distinguished in 16: 1–2. 'Beth-aven', which means 'house of Taboo', seems to be an insulting substitute for Bethel (see comment on 7: 2).

Beth-emek   (Tell Mīmās). 19: 27. Map 5.

Beth-hoglah   Must have been located in the vicinity of Deir Ḥajlah and 'Ain Ḥajlah. 15: 6; 18: 19, 21. Maps 3, 4.

Beth-horon   Upper and Lower Beth-horon may be identified, respectively, with Beit 'Ūr el-Fōqā and Beit 'Ūr et-Taḥtā. 10: 10; 16: 3–5; 18: 13–14; 21: 22. Maps 1, 4, 6.

Beth-jesimoth   (Tell el-'Aẓeimeh). 12: 3; 13: 20. Map 1.

Bethlehem   (Beit Laḥm). 19: 15. Map 5. To be distinguished from the Bethlehem in Judah (15: 59; supplied by the Septuagint).

Beth-shean   (Tell el-Ḥuṣn near Beisān). 17: 11, 16. Maps 1, 5.

Beth-shemesh   (Tell er-Rumeileh near 'Ain Shems). 15: 10; 19: 22, 38; 21: 16. Ir-shemesh in 19: 41 is an alternate name for the same city. Maps 4, 6.

Beth-Tappuah   (Taffūḥ). 15: 53. Map 3.

Beth-zur   (Khirbet eṭ-Ṭubeiqeh). 15: 58. Map 3.

Betonim   (Khirbet Baṭneh, approximately 10 kms (6 miles) south-west of es-Salṭ). 13: 26. Map 1.

Bezer   (possibly Umm el-'Amad). 20: 8. Map 6.

Cabul   (Kābūl). 19: 27. Map 5.

Cain   (en-Nebī Yaqīn). 15: 57. Map 3.

Carem   Ancient Carem must have been located in the vicinity of present-day 'Ain Kārim, approximately 5 kms (3 miles) west-by-south-west of Jerusalem. Some would identify it with Khirbet Ṣāliḥ (Ramat Raḥel). 15: 59 (Septuagint). Map 3.

Carmel   (Khirbet el-Kirmil). 15: 55. Map 3.

Dabbesheth   (possibly Tell esh-Shammām). 19: 11. Map 5.

Daberath   (Dabūriyeh at the foot of Mount Tabor). 19: 12; 21: 28. Maps 5, 6.

Debir   It is apparent from 10: 38–9; 11: 21; and 15: 13–19, 49 that Debir was located in the hill-country not far from Hebron. Scholars have tended to favour its identification with Tell Beit Mirsim, especially since 1926–32 when Tell Beit Mirsim was excavated and found to have been occupied more or less continuously from the Bronze Age throughout the Iron Age. This identification has been challenged in recent years, however, and seems increasingly unlikely. The biblical writers may themselves have had some uncertainties concerning Debir. Note that it is equated with Kiriath-sepher in 15: 15, but with Kiriath-sannah in 15: 49. In addition to the passage cited above, Debir appears in 10: 3; 12: 13; 21: 15. Maps 1, 2, 6. 15: 7 refers to another unidentified Debir on Judah's northern boundary.

Dibon (Dhibān). Site of the discovery of the 'Mesha Inscription' (see comment on 13:9). 13:9, 17. Maps 1, 2.

Dor See commentary on 12:23. There were at least two villages named 'Dor' in ancient Palestine. The most famous one, to which 11:2 probably refers, was situated on the Mediterranean coast and is probably to be associated with Khirbet el-Burj. Maps 1, 2, 5. 12:23 ; 17:11 and 21:32 probably refer to another Dor which must have been located in the vicinity of present-day 'En Dor. Maps 2, 5, 6.

Dumah (Khirbet Dōmeh ed-Deir). 15:52. Map 3.

Eder See Arad.

Edrei (Derʿā). 12:4; 13:12, 31; 19:37. Map 2.

Eglon (probably Tell el-Ḥesī). 10:3ff.; 12:12; 15:39. Maps 1, 2, 3.

Ekron (probably Khirbet el-Muqannaʿ). One of five Philistine cities listed in 13:3. See also 15:11, 45-6; 19:43. For the names and possible locations of the other four Philistine cities see entry under 'Ashdod'. Maps 1, 4.

Eltekeh/Eltekon We learn from the Assyrian records that Eltekeh was situated near Ekron (Khirbet el-Muqannaʿ) and Timnah (probably Tell el-Baṭāshī), both of which were situated on the southern side of Nahal Sorek, which seems to correspond roughly to the tribal boundary between Judah and Dan. Eltekeh must also have been located near this boundary, but probably on the Dan side. 15:59; 19:44; 21:23. Map 4.

En-gannim (Jenin). 19:21; 21:29. To be distinguished from the En-gannim in the Shephelah (15:34). Maps 5, 6.

En-gedi The ancient name is preserved in that of 'En Gedi (Arab. 'Ain Jidī) on the western bank of the Dead Sea. The Old Testament site is probably nearby Tell Goren. 15:62. Map 3.

En-haddah (name preserved in Karm el-Ḥadatheh, approximately 10 kms (6 miles) east of Mount Tabor). 19:21. Map 5.

Ephrathah/Bethlehem (Beit Laḥm). 15:59 (Septuagint). Map 3. To be distinguished from the Bethlehem in Zebulun (19:15).

Eshtaol (Ishwaʿ). 15:33; 19:41. Map 4.

Eshtemoh/Eshtemoa (es-Semūʿ). 15:50; 21:14. Maps 3, 6.

Etam (Khirbet el-Khōkh near 'Ain 'Aṭān). 15:59 (Septuagint). Map 3.

Ether (Khirbet el-ʿAter). 15:42; 19:7. Map 3.

Gallim Exact location uncertain, but Isa. 10:30 places it north-east of Jerusalem. 15:59 (Septuagint).

Gath One of the five Philistine cities enumerated in 13:3. See also 11:22. Location uncertain. Tell eṣ-Ṣāfi, 19 kms (approximately 12 miles) east of Ashdod seems a likely possibility. But some scholars would identify Tell eṣ-Ṣāfi as Libnah. For the names and probable

locations of the other four Philistine cities, see entry under 'Ashdod'.
Map 1.

Gath-hepher (Khirbet ez-Zurra', approximately 5 kms (3 miles) north-east of Nazareth). 19: 13. Map 5.

Gath-rimmon (probably Tell Jarīsheh). 19: 45; 21: 24. Read Ibleam instead of Gath-rimmon in 21: 25 with 1 Chron. 6: 69 and the Septuagint. Maps 4, 6.

Gaza (el-Ghazzeh). One of the five Philistine cities enumerated in 13: 3. See also 10: 41 and 15: 47. For the names and probable locations of the other four Philistine cities, see entry under 'Ashdod'. Map 1.

Geba (Jeba'). 18: 24; 21: 17. Maps 3, 4, 6.

Geder/Gedor (Khirbet Jedūr in the hill-country north of Beth-zur). 12: 13; 15: 58. Maps 2, 3. To be distinguished from Gederah, which was located in district II of the Judaean city list (15: 36).

Gederah (Khirbet Jedīreh, on the edge of the Valley of Aijalon). 15: 36. Map 3. To be distinguished from Geder/Gedor, which was situated in district VIII of the Judaean city list (15: 58).

Gezer (Tell Jezer). The identification of Tell Jezer as the site of ancient Gezer has been confirmed by the discovery of a series of rock inscriptions on the outskirts of the ruins which include the words 'boundary of Gezer'. 10: 33; 12: 12; 16: 3, 10; 21: 21. Maps 1, 2, 4, 6.

Gibbethon (probably Tell Melāt). 19: 44; 21: 23. Map 6.

Gibeon (el-Jīb). 9–10; 11: 19; 18: 25; 21: 17. Maps 1, 3, 4, 6.

Gilgal Must have been located immediately to the east of Jericho (cp. especially 4: 19). Earlier scholars were inclined to identify it with Khirbet en-Nītleh, which is situated approximately 4 kms (2¼ miles) east of modern Jericho; but Khirbet Mefjir, which is situated approximately 2 kms (1¼ miles) from the ancient site of Jericho (Tell es-Sulṭān), has been favoured more recently. 4: 19–20; 5: 9–10; 9: 6; 10: 6–7, 9, 15, 43; 14: 6. Map 1. The Hebrew texts refer to Gilgal in 12: 23 and 15: 7. But the versions supply variant readings, and in neither case can the Gilgal near Jericho have been intended.

Golan (possibly Saḥm el-Jōlān in Bashan). 20: 8; 21: 27. Map 6.

Halhul (Ḥalḥūl). 15: 58. Map 3.

Hammath (Ḥāmmam Ṭabarīyeh). 19: 35. Probably mentioned again in 21: 32 (see commentary). Maps 5, 6.

Hammon (Umm el-'Awāmīd). 19: 28. Map 5.

Hammoth-dor 21: 32. Should probably be read as two different cities – i.e. Hammoth and Dor. Hammoth appears again in 19: 35 as Hammath, and is to be identified with Ḥāmmam Ṭabarīyeh. This is probably the same Dor to which 12: 23 and 17: 11 refer (see commentary on 21: 32). Map 6.

Hannathon (possibly Tell el-Bedeiwiyeh). 19: 14. Map 5.

Hazor (Tell el-Qedaḥ). 11: 1ff.; 12: 19. Maps 1, 2, 5.

Hebron (Jebel er-Rumēde near el-Khalīl). 10: 3ff.; 11: 21; 12: 10; 14: 13–15; 15: 13, 54; 20: 7; 21: 11–13. Maps 1, 2, 3. See Kiriath-arba.

Heleph (possibly Khirbet 'Irbādeh). 19: 33. Map 5.

Hepher Appears only in 12: 17 and 1 Kings 4: 10, the latter of which describes Solomon's third district: 'Ben-hesed in Aruboth; he had charge also of Socoh and all the land of Hepher.' The names 'Aruboth' and 'Hepher' may be preserved in those of the present-day village 'Arrāba and Khirbet el-Hafireh about 3 kms (approximately 2 miles) to the east. Ancient Hepher must have been somewhere in the vicinity. Map 2.

Heshbon (Ḥesbān). 9: 10; 12: 2–5; 13: 10ff.; 21: 39. Maps 2, 6.

Hormah Located in the Negeb. Tell el-Milḥ and Khirbet el-Meshāsh have been proposed, both of which are located on the Wadi Meshāsh south-west of Arad. 12: 14; 15: 30; 19: 4. Maps 2, 3.

Hosah 19: 29. Possibly to be equated with the mainland portion of Tyre, called 'Uzu' in the Egyptian and Assyrian records, 'Palaityros' in hellenistic texts and 'Tell Rashīdīyeh' by the local population today. Asher's northern boundary is problematic in any case if 'the fortress city of Tyre' is to be identified as the island portion of the city – i.e. we are told that the boundary extended 'as far as the fortress city of Tyre, and then back again to Hosah'. It has been suggested that 'the fortress city of Tyre' also refers to the mainland suburb and that the verse be translated as follows: 'Then the boundary turns to Ramah reaching the fortified city of Tyre [which is] Hosah, and it ends in the sea.' Map 5.

Ibleam (Khirbet Bel'ameh). 17: 11. Should be read instead of Gath-rimmon in 21: 25 (cp. 1 Chron. 6: 69). Maps 5, 6.

Ir-melach (probably Khirbet Qumran). 15: 62. The name means 'city of Salt'. Map 3.

Iron/Yiron (Yārūm). 19: 38. Map 5.

Jabneel (Yebnā). 15: 11. Map 4. To be distinguished from the Jabneel in Naphtali (19: 33).

Jahaz Situated on the edge of the 'wilderness' just north of the Arnon. Several sites have been proposed. Khirbet 'Aleiyān is perhaps the strongest candidate. 13: 18; 21: 37. Map 6.

Janoah (Khirbet Yānūn). 16: 6–7. Map 4.

Japhia (Yāfā). 19: 12. Map 5.

Jarmuth (Khirbet el-Yarmūk). 10: 3ff.; 12: 11; 15: 35. Maps 1, 2, 3.

Jashub This reading in 17: 7 requires a slight textual emendation. The name seems to be preserved in that of the present-day village, Yāsūf, located near the sources of the Wadi Qānah. Map 4.

Jattir (Khirbet 'Attīr). 15: 48; 21: 14. Maps 3, 6.

Jazer Located in the highlands north of Heshbon and, according to the Septuagint version of Num. 21: 24, situated on the Ammonite frontier. Several sites have been proposed. 13: 25; 21: 39. Map 6.

Jebus/the Jebusite 15: 8; 18: 16, 28. Equated with Jerusalem in 15: 8; 18: 28; and Judg. 19: 10. Compare also 1 Chron. 11: 4 with 2 Sam. 5: 6. However this equation is open to serious question. Jebus may have been a separate village located slightly further north, possibly in the vicinity of present-day Shu'fāt (see commentary on 15: 8, 59, 63; 18: 28). Maps 3, 4.

Jehud (el-Yehūdīyeh). 19: 45. Map 4.

Jericho (Tell es-Sulṭān). Jericho is referred to throughout chs. 2–10. See also 12: 9; 13: 32; 16: 1, 7; 18: 12, 21; 20: 8; 24: 11. Maps 1, 2, 3, 4.

Jerusalem 10: 1ff.; 12: 10; 15: 8, 63; 18: 28. Maps 1, 2, 3, 4. See Jebus.

Jezreel (Zer'īn, 7 kms (4 miles) south-east of 'Affuleh). 17: 16; 19: 18. Map 5. To be distinguished from the Jezreel of the Judaean hill-country (15: 56).

Jokneam (Tell Qeimūn). 12: 22; 19: 11; 21: 34. Appears as 'Jokmeam' in 1 Kings 4: 12 and 1 Chron. 6: 68. Both 19: 11 and 21: 34 mention Jokneam in connection with Zebulun, although 19: 11 implies that it lay just outside Zebulun's territorial limits. Maps 2, 5, 6.

Joppa (Yāfā). 19: 46. Map 4.

Juttah (Yaṭṭā). 15: 55; 21: 16. Maps 3, 6.

Kadesh-barnea The ancient name seems to be preserved in that of 'Ain Qedeis, one of several springs located on the southern edge of the Negeb. 10: 41; 14: 6–7; 15: 3. Map 1. Whether the Kedesh in 15: 23 is Kedesh-barnea is uncertain.

Kanah (Qānā). 19: 28. Map 5.

Kedemoth Deut. 2: 26 places Kedemoth on the south-eastern frontier of Sihon's kingdom, which would imply that it was situated in the upper Arnon. Qaṣr ez-Za'feran or Khirbet er-Remeil, both of which are located in that vicinity and were occupied during the Iron Age, are possibilities. 13: 18; 21: 37. Map 6.

Kedesh Several villages went by this name, which indicated a 'sanctuary' or 'holy place'. Perhaps the most prominent was 'Kedesh in Galilee', which is identified as a city of refuge and a Levitical city in Naphtali (20: 7; 21: 32. Probably Tell Qades north of Hazor. Map 6). 19: 37 may refer to this same Kedesh, or to another located near Naphtali's southern boundary (see comment on 19: 33–4a. Khirbet el-Qadīsh on the south-west shore of the Sea of Galilee would be a possibility). The Kedesh mentioned in 12: 22 is associated there with other cities in the northern Ephraimite hill-country, and may have been located in the vicinity of Tell Abū Qudēs between Taanach and Megiddo (Map 2). The Kedesh mentioned in 15:23 belongs to the Negeb district of the Judaean city list, and may be identical with Kadesh-barnea.

Keilah (Khirbet Qīlā). 15:44. Map 3.

Kephirah (Khirbet el-Kefīreh). 9:17; 18:26. Maps 1, 3.

Kesulloth/Kisloth-tabor Probably located in the vicinity of present-day Iksāl. 19:12, 18. Map 5.

Kiriath-arba Kiriath-arba appears twice in the patriarchal narratives (Gen. 23:2; 35:27); its conquest is attributed to Caleb in Josh. 15:13; it is listed in the sixth district of the Judahite city list (15:54); and appears as a Levitical city of refuge in 20:7; 21:11. In each of these cases a scribal notation has been introduced into the text which identifies Kiriath-arba as Hebron. The situation is reversed in 14:15 (paralleled by Judg. 1:10) – i.e. in this case it is Hebron which has been identified secondarily as Kiriath-arba, with the explanation that Kiriath-arba was an earlier name for the city. This explanation is problematic on at least two counts: (1) the name 'Hebron' appears in some of the older strata of the Old Testament; (2) there was a village still going by the name Kiriath-arba as late as the post-exilic period (see Neh. 11:25). Thus the connection between Kiriath-arba and Hebron remains unclear. Maps 1, 2, 3, 6.

Kiriath-baal/Kiriath-jearim The relationship between Baalah, Kiriath-baal, Kiriath-jearim, Mount Jearim, and Gibeath Kiriath-jearim is unclear (see commentary on 15:6–11 and 18:25–8). All must have been related in some fashion to Kiriath-jearim, however, which is probably to be associated with Deir el-ʿAzar near Abū Ghōsh. Maps 1, 3, 4.

Kishion (Khirbet Qasyūn). 19:20; 21:28. Maps 5, 6.

Lachish (Tell ed-Duweir). 10: 3ff.; 12:11; 15:39. Maps 1, 2, 3.

Lebo-hamath The ideal northern limit of Israel's territorial possessions. Location uncertain. The pass between the Lebanon and the Anti-Lebanon Mountains at Baʿalbek would seem to be a likely natural boundary; and the name 'Lebo' may be preserved in that of present day 'Lebweh' which is situated at the northern entrance to the valley. 13:5. Map 1.

Libnah Often associated with Tell eṣ-Ṣāfi, but there is reason now to believe that Tell eṣ-Ṣāfi was 'Gath of the Philistines'. Tell Bornāṭ is a likely alternative. 10: 29ff.; 12:15; 15:42; 21:13. Maps 1, 2, 6.

Luz See 'Bethel'.

Madmannah (Khirbet Umm ed-Deimneh). 15:31. Map 3.

Madon (Khirbet Midyan on Qarn Ḥaṭṭin). 11:1; 12:19. Maps 1, 2.

Mahanaim The biblical data seem to place Mahanaim near the Jordan (2 Sam. 2:29; 17:24), and apparently near the Jabbok (Gen. 32).

It has been identified with Tulul edh-Dhahab, but this now seems unlikely. The name may be preserved in that of Khirbet Maḥneh, not far from the village of Ajlūn. 13: 26, 30; 21: 38. Map 6.

Makkedah   Location uncertain. Khirbet Maqdūm has been proposed on the basis of the *Onomastikon* of Eusebius, the church historian (A.D. 260–340). Note that it was in the same administrative district as Lachish and Eglon. 10: 10ff.; 12: 16; 15: 41. Maps 1, 2.

Manach   (el-Malḥah). 15: 59 (Septuagint). Map 3.

Maon   (Khirbet Maʻīn). 15: 55. Map 3.

Mareshah   (Tell Ṣandaḥannah). 15: 44. Map 3.

Medeba   (Mādeba). 13: 9, 16. The memorial inscription erected by King Mesha of Moab during the ninth century B.C. seems to distinguish between 'the district of Dibon' – i.e. the plateau between the Wadi el-Mūjib (Arnon) and the Wadi el-Ḥeidān – and 'the land of Medeba' – i.e. the tableland north of the Wadi el-Ḥeidān, especially the fertile area surrounding Medeba, but apparently not extending as far as Heshbon. Map 1.

Megiddo   (Tell el-Mutesellim). 12: 21; 17: 11. Maps 1, 2, 5.

Michmethath   In the immediate vicinity of Shechem (Tell Balāṭah), but cannot be located more precisely. 16: 6; 17: 7. Map 4.

Middin, Secacah, Nibshan   Probably to be identified with three Iron Age sites which have been discovered in the el-Beqeiʻa region: Khirbet Abū Ṭabaq, Khirbet es-Samrah, and Khirbet el-Maqārī. 15: 61. Map 3.

Mizpah/Mizpeh   Two different Mizpahs appear in the Judaean city list, one is district II (15: 38, location uncertain) and one is district X (18: 26; probably Tell en-Naṣbeh; Maps 3, 4). Note also the reference to 'the land of Mizpah' and 'the Vale of Mizpah' in the vicinity of 'Greater Sidon' and Mount Hermon (11: 3, 8); and Ramoth-mizpeh in the Transjordan (13: 26). It is uncertain whether the latter is identical with the Mizpeh of the Jephthah episode, which was also located in the Transjordan (Judg. 10: 17ff.). Mizpah means 'watchtower'.

Naarath   Location uncertain; possibly Khirbet el-ʻAyāsh. Eusebius places it 5 Roman miles (roughly 7 kms or 4½ modern miles) north of Jericho. 16: 7. Map 4.

Nahalal   (Tell en-Nahl). 19: 15; 21: 35. Maps 5, 6.

Neiel   (Khirbet Yaʻnīn). 19: 27. Map 5.

Nezib   (Khirbet Beit Neṣīb). 15: 43. Map 3.

Nibshan   See Middin.

Ophrah   (eṭ-Ṭaiyibeh). 18: 23. Map 3.

Parah   (Tell el-Fārah near the spring ʻAin Fārah and Wadi Fārah). 18: 23. Map 3.

Peor (Khirbet Fāghūr). 15: 59 (Septuagint). Map 3.

Rabbah/Rabbath-ammon ('Ammān). 13: 25. To be distinguished from the Rabbah which appears in the Judaean city list (15: 60). Map 1.

Ramah Five cities by this name appear in the book of Joshua: (1) Ramah in district X of the Judaean city list (18: 25, present-day er-Rām, Maps 3, 4); (2) Ramah in Simeon, i.e. Ramath-negeb (19: 8); (3) Ramah in Asher (19: 29); (4) Ramah in Naphtali (19: 36, probably Khirbet Zeitūn er-Rāmeh, Map 5); (5) Ramah in Gilead – i.e. Ramoth-gilead (21: 38, Tell Rāmīth, Map 6). The name means 'height'.

Rehob (possibly Tell el-Bīr el-Gharbī). 19: 28, 30; 21: 31. Maps 5, 6.

Rimmon (Rummāneh). 19: 13. Maps 5, 6. Note also the 'Ain' and 'Rimmon' assigned to Judah (15: 32) and Simeon (19: 7). This should probably be read as a single name, 'En-rimmon', in both places. It is often identified with Khirbet er-Ramāmīn, approximately 15 kms (9 miles) north-by-north-east of Beer-sheba.

Salcah (Ṣalkhad). 12: 5; 13: 11. Map 1.

Sansannah (Khirbet esh-Shamsanīyāt). 15: 31. Map 3.

Secacah See Middin.

Shaalabbin (Selbīt). 19: 42. Map 4.

Shadud 19: 10, 12. The Hebrew text reads 'Sarid'. Probably to be identified with Tell Shadūd, 7 kms (4 miles) south-west of Nazareth. Map 5.

Sharuhen/Shilhim Compare 15: 32 with 19: 6. It is tempting, on the basis of the similarity in names, to associate Sharuhen with Tell esh-Sharī'ah, which is located south-east of Gaza. The results of archaeological excavations at nearby Tell el-Fār'ah, however, strongly suggest it as the site of ancient Sharuhen. Map 3.

Shechem (Tell Balāṭah near Nablus). 17: 7; 20: 7; 21: 21; 24: 1ff. Maps 1, 4, 6.

Shilhim See Sharuhen. Probably Tell el-Fār'ah. Map 3.

Shiloh (Khirbet Seilūn). 18: 1ff.; 19: 51; 21: 2; 22: 9, 12. Maps 1, 4.

Shimron/Shimron-meron The designation 'meron' was probably introduced into the list of conquered cities (12: 20) in order to distinguish this Shimron – which was apparently located in the vicinity of 'the waters of Meron' (see also 11: 1–5, Maps 1, 2) – from the Shimron in Zebulun (19: 15, Map 5), and possibly from Samaria (Hebrew 'Shomron').

Shittim Must have been located near the Jordan opposite Jericho, and probably to be equated with Abel-shittim (cp. Num. 33: 49). Has been identified variously with Tell el-Kefrein and Tell el-Ḥammām, both of which are in that vicinity. 2: 1; 3: 1. Map 1.

Shunem (Sōlem, 5 kms (3 miles) east of 'Affuleh). 19: 18. Map 5.

Socoh   Two different towns by this name appear in the Judaean city list: one in district II (probably Khirbet 'Abbād) and one in district V (Khirbet Shuweikeh). 15: 36, 48. Map 3.

Succoth   (probably Tell Deir 'Allā). 13: 27. Map 1.

Taanach   (Tell Ti'innik). 12: 21; 17: 11; 21: 25. Maps 2, 5, 6.

Taanath-shiloh   Location uncertain, but it must have been located in the vicinity of Shechem and Janoah. See comments on 16: 6–7, and 17: 7–10a. The name may be preserved in that of Khirbet Ta'nā, approximately 12 kms (7 miles) south-east of Shechem (Tell Balāṭah) and 3 kms (2 miles) north of Janoah (Yānūn). Map 4.

Tappuah/En-tappuah   Probably to be identified with Tell esh-Sheikh Abū Zarad, but this is not entirely certain. 12: 17; 16: 8; 17: 7–8. Maps 2, 4. To be distinguished from another Tappuah which was located in the second Shephelah district of the Judaean city list (15: 34).

Tekoa   (Khirbet Teqū'). 15: 59 (Septuagint). Map 3.

Timnah   Usually identified with Khirbet Tibnah, about 4 kms (2½ miles) south-west of Beth-shemesh. It now appears doubtful, however, that Khirbet Tibnah was occupied prior to Roman times. Perhaps a more likely site for ancient Timnah is Tell el-Baṭāshī, approximately 5 kms (3 miles) to the north-west of Khirbet Tibnah on the edge of Nahal Sorek. 15: 10; 19: 43. Map 4. This Timnah is to be distinguished from the one which appears in district VII of the Judaean city list (15: 57) and Timnath-serah (see entry below). The name probably means 'allotted portion'.

Timnath-serah   (Khirbet Tibneh). 19: 50; 24: 30. Same as Timnath-heres in Judg. 2: 9. Map 1.

Tirzah   (Tell el-Fār'ah). 12: 24. Map 2.

Tyre   (eṣ-Ṣūr). 19: 29. See entry under 'Hosah'. Map 5.

Zanoah   (Khirbet Zānū'). 15: 34. Map 3. To be distinguished from another Zanoah in district VII of the Judaean city list (15: 56).

Zaphon   Possibly Tell es-Sa'īdīyeh – which, however, has been identified by some scholars as Zerathan. 13: 27. Map 1.

Ziph   (Tell Zīf). 15: 55. Map 3. To be distinguished from another Ziph in district I of the Judaean city list (15: 24).

Zorah   (Ṣar'ah). 15: 33; 19: 41. Maps 3, 4.

INDEX

Only those Palestinian place-names which figure prominently in the narrative portions of Joshua are included in the index. Consult also the list of 'Geographical Terms in Joshua' and the 'Gazetteer'.